ADULT SAFEGUARDING

How Social Work
Risk and

Jeremy Dixon

P

First published in Great Britain in 2023 by

Policy Press, an imprint of
Bristol University Press
University of Bristol
1–9 Old Park Hill
Bristol
BS2 8BB
UK
t: +44 (0)117 374 6645
e: bup-info@bristol.ac.uk

Details of international sales and distribution partners are available at
policy.bristoluniversitypress.co.uk

British Library Cataloguing in Publication Data
A catalogue record for this book is available from the British Library

ISBN 978-1-4473-5728-5 hardcover
ISBN 978-1-4473-5729-2 paperback
ISBN 978-1-4473-5730-8 ePub
ISBN 978-1-4473-5731-5 ePdf

Cover design: Liam Roberts Design
Front cover image: iStock/SilviaJansen

To the women in my life – Susannah, Bibi and my Mum.

Contents

List of abbreviations   vi
Acknowledgements   vii

Introduction   1

1   The problem of adult safeguarding   16

2   Risk and social work   36

3   Referrals and assessments   59

4   Personalised safeguarding: policy, principles and practice realities   81

5   Doing adult safeguarding with service users and carers   99

Conclusion   126

Notes   138
References   140
Index   159

List of abbreviations

ADASS	Association of Directors of Adult Social Services
ADSS	Association of Directors of Social Services
AEGIS	Aid for the Elderly in Government Institutions
ARC	Association for Residential Care
CQC	Care Quality Commission
DHSC	Department of Health and Social Care
ICT	information and communications technology
LGA	Local Government Association
NAPSAC	National Association for the Protection from Sexual Abuse of Adults and Children with Learning Disabilities
NHS	National Health Service

Acknowledgements

First and foremost, I would like to thank the social workers who took time to talk to me about their work and allowed me to observe them as part of my research. Thanks also to the team managers in the three local authorities where the research was carried out for their enthusiasm in the project and for enabling me to gain access to their staff.

Several people kindly read and commented on draft chapters. A big thank you to Patrick Brown, Daniel Burrows, Emma Carmel, Hazel Kemshall, Jill Manthorpe, Megan Robb, Kate Spreadbury, Diana Teggi, Tony Walter and Joanne Warner for this. I would also like to thank the anonymous reviewers who commented on the proposal and the full draft.

I am indebted to Isobel Bainton, my editor at Policy Press. Your help and patience throughout the project were appreciated. A big shout to Sarah Day, Angela Gage, Vicky Delahunty and Jay Allan at Policy Press for their work on the book.

Introduction

Why focus on adult safeguarding?

This book focuses on how social workers understand adult safeguarding and how they conduct duties related to this. Since the introduction of the Care Act 2014, adult safeguarding has begun to have a higher profile within the literature on social work in England – some would argue, not before time. The *Care and Support Statutory Guidance* for England describes safeguarding as a process which protects 'an adult's right to live in safety, free from abuse and neglect' (Department of Health and Social Care – DHSC, 2022, para 14.7). It involves 'people and organisations working together to prevent and stop both the risks and experience of abuse or neglect, while at the same time making sure that the adult's wellbeing is promoted including, where appropriate, having regard to their views, wishes, feelings and beliefs in deciding on any action' (DHSC, 2022, para 14.7). I describe the key duties for local authorities and discuss who safeguarding duties apply to later in this chapter. Before doing so, I want to set out the broad aims for this book.

What this book is about

This book does three things. First, it is a book about adult safeguarding. Within its chapters, I report on a research project carried out in three local authorities in England. The aim of my research was to explore how front-line social workers assess and manage adult safeguarding risks. When looking at this issue, I was interested in the following questions:

- How do social workers interpret safeguarding duties as laid out by the Care Act 2014?
- What sources of information do social workers draw on when assessing and managing adult safeguarding risks?
- How do agency policies, procedures and cultures influence the way in which social workers assess and manage risk?
- To what extent are the views of service users themselves considered within safeguarding assessments?

Second, this is a book about risk in social work practice. Throughout the book, I attempt to unpack what we mean when we talk about risk and how we seek to manage it. I use sociological theories of risk and uncertainty to think about adult safeguarding practice. From speaking to social work students and practitioners over the years, I am aware that theory is often viewed by them as something which is dusty, dry or difficult, or as having little relevance 'on the ground'. If you are a reader who is not interested in theory, you may want to skip the theory chapter. However, it is my hope that readers will engage with the theory in this book. Doing theory can be like doing exercise. It can often feel like hard work to start with, but it has long-term benefits. Teaching social work has taught me that students and practitioners report benefits from thinking about theory, namely the ability to see what they are doing from a fresh perspective and to improve their practice.

Third, the book charts the development of social policy relating to adult safeguarding in England and shows how it came to be seen as a social problem. The term 'adult safeguarding' is a relatively recent one, so I show how concerns about adult abuse and neglect grew over time, leading to the current law and policy. Adult safeguarding policy is likely to go through further developments. My research helps to highlight which aspects of law and policy are valued by social work practitioners and which are seen as problematic. In the concluding chapter, I make suggestions as to how safeguarding policy might be developed.

Safeguarding involves working with adults who are experiencing different forms of abuse and neglect. The book contains material in which social workers speak of situations where people they are working with are experiencing or suspected of experiencing abuse or neglect. This includes physical abuse, sexual abuse, domestic violence, emotional abuse, discrimination and self-neglect.

Thinking about risk

I became interested in the topic of risk first as a practitioner and then later as an academic. Most of my time as a social worker was spent working in mental health teams of one sort or another. While I was working in a mental health team in Bristol, my manager told me that I was "good with working with risk". By this, he meant that I was good at weighing up the benefits of risk taking, from the perspective of the people we were working with, as well as thinking about what might be done to minimise risk. Although I was pleased to receive this compliment, I was not sure I deserved it. As a mental health worker, I was aware that we needed to allow the people we were working with to take risks if they were to progress; this process is often referred to in the literature as 'positive risk taking' (Titterton, 2004, 2011). However, I also experienced a lot of anxiety about risk. Several practitioners I knew had been hauled up in front of mental health inquiries when they had been involved in cases where individuals with mental health problems had died or harmed others. I certainly didn't want to be in this position and worried about whether the risks I had taken were defensible. I was careful to document my practice whenever I took a risk and to show where I had shared my decisions with other professionals. However, this took a lot of time and so I also worried about being overly defensive. Would the time I was spending recording these risks have been better spent elsewhere, and was this process causing me to be risk-averse?

My academic interest in risk began when I started my professional doctorate in social work. By this time, I was working in a medium secure unit with offenders who had mental health problems and had committed serious offences. Discussion about a person's offending risk, their risk to others or risk to themselves was a regular feature of ward rounds and care planning meetings. What was peculiar about these conversations was that they usually took place among professionals when the service user was absent. When the service user joined the meeting, the discussions would be reframed, focusing on therapy, treatment and 'things we are doing to help you' – an indirect way of talking about medication, monitoring and aftercare. Furthermore, staff often avoided talking to service users about risk, either because they assumed that someone else would do it or because they were worried about the person becoming angry or upset. I found it problematic that we understood little about what service users thought. This led me to undertake a doctorate examining what service users thought about their own offending risks (Dixon, 2018), risk assessments (see Dixon, 2012) and supervision in the community (Dixon, 2015).

Risk is a topic which has been written about in the social work literature a lot. As I outline in Chapter 2, several authors in this field have written theoretically about risk, most notably Hazel Kemshall (2001, 2010, 2013, 2016) and Stephen Webb (2006, 2009). There have also been many studies on social workers' understanding of the concept of risk and how they work with it in practice. However, most of these studies were conducted in children and family, mental health or probation settings. I therefore began to wonder how safeguarding work was organised and how duties to safeguard adults at risk were understood and operationalised.

It is useful to set out some of the preconceptions I held before beginning my research. As Delamont (1992) notes, when starting a research study, preconceptions are not bad in themselves. Rather, the danger lies in preconceptions remaining 'implicit, unacknowledged, and unexamined' (Delamont, 1992, p 77). As a practitioner, most of my practice experience had been in multidisciplinary mental health teams. I had experience of conducting mental health assessments under the Mental Health Act 1983 (as amended by the Mental Health Act 2007), which is a form of adult safeguarding. However, I had little experience of working within social work adult community teams, which promote the independence and wellbeing of adults more generally. My expectations of how these teams worked came from my discussions with adult social workers and managers when teaching a post-qualifying course to adult social workers from 2009 to 2012. Several themes arose in these discussions. Social workers identified uncertainty about how they should assess safeguarding concerns. Reflecting the guidance of the time (Department of Health, 2000), social workers wondered who should be regarded as a 'vulnerable adult' and how they might measure or monitor risks. Social workers struggled with dilemmas about which service users should be empowered to take risks and which ones should be discouraged or prevented from doing so. They also worried about how to interpret government guidance, often feeling that they had few powers to draw on. Many felt pressured by their managers to close cases quickly and worried that, as a result, little support would be given to service users to manage identified risks. These accounts informed my preconceptions about adult safeguarding, and I expected some of these issues to arise in my research. As we will see, while some of these themes were reflected in my research data, I also found that social workers' concerns are broader and more complex than this.

Adult safeguarding duties under the Care Act 2014

This book focuses on how adult social workers assess and manage adult safeguarding risks. In the next chapter, I set out how adult safeguarding came to be seen as a social problem (Blumer, 1971; Best, 2013) and the steps the government has taken to address it in England. I give a detailed account of how safeguarding laws and policies have developed. However, I am aware that adult safeguarding may not be familiar territory to all, so I briefly describe current law and policy here.

Section 1 of the Care Act 2014 states that every local authority has a duty to promote individual wellbeing, which includes protection from abuse and neglect. Where a safeguarding referral is made, practitioners acting on behalf of the local authority must consider their duties under sections 42–46 of the Care Act 2014, which state that:

- Every local authority should establish a Safeguarding Adults Board, which should lead safeguarding arrangements across the locality and coordinate safeguarding work across partner agencies.
- Safeguarding Adults Boards should arrange for safeguarding adults reviews to take place in cases where there are concerns about how members of the Safeguarding Adults Boards, or other professionals, have worked together to safeguard an individual.
- Local authorities should make enquiries where a concern is raised about an adult in their area (whether they normally live there or not) to establish whether action should be taken to prevent or stop abuse and neglect.

Section 42(1) of the Care Act 2014 states that local authorities' duties to undertake safeguarding enquiries apply where an adult:

(a) has needs for care and support (whether or not the authority is meeting any of those needs),
(b) is experiencing, or is at risk of, abuse or neglect, and
(c) as a result of those needs is unable to protect himself or herself against the abuse or neglect or the risk of it

People who are referred to adult safeguarding services have a wide range of care and support needs. They may have poor health or a physical disability. They may have a learning disability, autism, a mental health problem or dementia, or be experiencing addiction problems. Or they may be a family carer for someone else with a care and support need. Adult safeguarding duties apply to people in the community and to those in institutions, such as care homes, psychiatric hospitals and secure units.

Where the Section 42 criteria are met, the local authority must make whatever enquiries it thinks necessary to enable it to decide whether any action should be taken in the adult's case and, if so, what and by whom. The local authority may cause another organisation to undertake the enquiry. For example, where abuse is alleged to have taken place in a provider service, such as a care home, the social worker in charge of the case may ask the manager of that care home to conduct an enquiry under the social worker's supervision. Safeguarding decisions may take place as a response to a specific enquiry or may occur as part of a general assessment of need. Enquiries should be conducted in line with the six safeguarding principles of the Care Act 2014, which are empowerment, protection, prevention, proportionality, partnership and accountability. The *Care and Support Statutory Guidance* highlights different types of abuse which individuals may experience, including physical abuse, domestic violence, sexual abuse, psychological abuse, financial or material abuse, modern slavery, discriminatory abuse, organisational abuse, neglect and acts of omission, and self-neglect (DHSC, 2022, para 14.17). This list is not intended to be exhaustive, and other types of abuse may be addressed under the Care Act 2014.

Since 2010, the Local Government Association (LGA) and the Association of Directors of Adult Social Services (ADASS) have worked to promote the Making Safeguarding Personal initiative (Ogilvie and Williams, 2010), which is endorsed in the *Care and Support Statutory Guidance* (DHSC, 2022, para 1.31). To implement the approach, the sector has produced a number of toolkits with the aim of making practice strengths-based and outcomes focused (see LGA and ADASS, 2019; Ogilvie and Williams, 2010; LGA, 2022b). In practice, this means having a conversation with the person the safeguarding enquiry is about and engaging with them to find ways to respond to the concern in a way which enhances their involvement, choice and control (LGA and ADASS, 2019).

Relevance of the Mental Capacity Act 2005

Many safeguarding decisions are affected by judgements about whether an adult has or lacks mental capacity. For this reason, the Mental Capacity Act 2005 is commonly referred to within safeguarding cases. There are five key principles to the Mental Capacity Act 2005, which are given in section 1 of that Act. These are:

- A person must be assumed to have capacity unless it is established that they lack capacity.
- A person should not be treated as unable to make a decision unless all practicable steps to help them to do so have been taken without success.
- A person should not be treated as unable to make a decision merely because they make an unwise decision.
- Decisions taken for people lacking capacity should always be made in their best interests.
- Before an act is done, or a decision is made on a person's behalf, consideration should be given about whether the outcome can be achieved in a less restrictive way.

Judgements about mental capacity are 'decision specific', meaning that a person may have the capacity to make judgements in one area, but not another. For example, a person may have capacity to make decisions about their care, but lack capacity to make decisions about their finances. Section 4 of the Act sets out issues that should be considered to ensure a person's best interests are met. These include:

(a) the person's past and present wishes and feelings (and, in particular, any relevant written statement made by him when he had capacity),
(b) the beliefs and values that would be likely to influence his decision if he had capacity, and
(c) the other factors that he would be likely to consider if he were able to do so. (Mental Capacity Act 2005, Section 4(6))

When deciding what is in a person's best interests, social workers, or other individuals must use the best interests checklist, which provides a comprehensive list of things to consider, including:

- the need to involve the person as much as possible, identifying their views and wishes (including what they would have wanted before they lost the capacity to make the decision);

- the need to respect the person's cultural and religious beliefs;
- the need to talk to people who know the person well, such as family and friends or care staff who have a good relationship with the person; and
- the need to limit any restrictions on the person.

The Mental Capacity Act 2005 also enables individuals to take out a lasting power of attorney. This is a legal document which states who the person would like to manage their property and finances once they lose capacity (sections 9–14). Furthermore, the Act allows for a person involved in an adult protection case to be supported by a independent mental capacity advocate where they lack capacity, even when the person has family or friends (Section 4 of the Mental Capacity Act 2005 (Independent Mental Capacity Advocates) (Expansion of Role) Regulations 2006).

These issues around mental capacity are relevant to decisions around risk, as the principle that a person should not be treated as unable to make a decision merely because they make an unwise decision applies. However, while the five principles exist in law, they may not always be applied as intended. For instance, as the House of Lords Select Committee on the Mental Capacity Act 2005 notes, '[t]he concept of unwise decision-making faces institutional obstruction due to prevailing cultures of risk-aversion and paternalism' (2014, para 104).

My approach to the research

To answer my research questions, I carried out observations of and interviews with social workers. In taking this approach, I drew on the principles of a research method called ethnography. The term 'ethnography' derives from the field of anthropology, with term 'ethno' referring to people or folk and 'graphy' referring to description (Punch, 2014). There are ongoing arguments about how ethnography should be defined. However, in its most characteristic form, it involves watching people's lives over an extended period of time, either overtly or covertly, listening to what is said and asking questions (Hammersley and Atkinson, 2019). When using ethnography, people's actions and accounts are studied within their everyday settings, with participant observation (where the researcher observes people of interest) and informal conversations being the central methods. The focus of ethnographic studies is normally on a particular workplace or setting. Observations and conversations are then analysed by the researcher to identify 'the meanings, sources, functions and consequences of social actions and institutional practices, and how these are implicated in local, and perhaps also wider, contexts' (Hammersley and Atkinson, 2019, p 3).

The research described in this book took place in three local authority social work departments in England, which I have named Fosborough,

Gainsborough and Almsbury to protect the confidentiality of local authorities and research participants.

Fosborough is an authority covering a large city area. It is more ethnically diverse than the national average for England and Wales (86 per cent of the national population were identified as White at the time of the study; Gov. uk, 2020b). The population of the city is young compared to the national average (nationally, 21.3 per cent of the population is under 18, 29.5 per cent are aged 18–39, 26.7 per cent are aged 40–59 and 22.5 per cent are aged 60 and above; Gov.uk, 2020a).

Gainsborough local authority is smaller, having a population just over half that of Fosborough. There is an urban/rural split in this local authority, with most living in urban areas. The population is less ethnically diverse than the national average. The age structure of Gainsborough is similar to the national average.

Finally, Almsbury has a population similar in size to that of Gainsborough. The population in this authority is equally spread between urban and rural areas. The population is less ethnically diverse than the national average. In terms of age, this authority has a higher proportion of adults aged 65 and above than the national average.

The research study received ethical approval through the Social Science Research Ethics Committee at the University of Bath and through local authority ethics committees in the Fosborough and Gainsborough. Almsbury did not have a research ethics committee, so permission was granted by the Director of Social Services. No payments were given to participants for taking part. The research was conducted between 2017 and 2019.

When designing this study, I was influenced by previous ethnographic research conducted in child protection (Scourfield, 2002; Pithouse, 2019) and mental health (Morriss, 2016a, 2017). These studies were valuable because they considered how social workers understood their role, the factors that affected their decision-making and how they were influenced by agency policies or culture. As these authors note, close descriptions of social work practice are not common in the research literature. For example, Pithouse (2019) refers to social work as an 'invisible trade', citing three reasons for this. First, many day-to-day interactions between social workers and their service users are carried out within the home or privately in the social work office. Second, the outcomes social workers are working toward often remain uncertain or ambiguous. Third, social workers do not routinely spend time analysing the processes they use when working with others. In line with the authors mentioned here, I thought that adopting an ethnographic approach would be a useful way of observing the minutia of day-to-day practice to gain insight into how risk was managed.

Negotiating access to social work participants can be tricky. Before research can begin, access needs to be granted by senior figures in the organisations where they work. Such individuals may worry that researchers pose a risk to their organisation. For example, ethnographic researchers in the social work field have been suspected of being an abuser (Scourfield and Coffey, 2006) or accused of 'spying' on the organisation (D'Cruz, 2004). In Fosborough I approached the principal social worker and safeguarding manager who were keen to help but had concerns that one of the organisation's directors might veto the research due to their concern about reputational damage. I was advised to submit a short proposal to them, which they would run by this director. Following this approach, I was asked by the principal social worker (who was clearly embarrassed by having to ask the question) if I would agree not to criticise the social workers in my research reports. I explained that I would have to describe safeguarding practice as I saw it, but would anonymise any data so that the identity of social workers or the local authority were not evident. To my surprise, access was agreed shortly after this exchange. The second and third local authorities I approached (Gainsborough and Almsbury) were happy to grant access. I provided managers in each authority with information sheets about the research, which they then gave to potential participants. Potential participants were informed about the purpose of the study and what it involved, and they were also advised that they were under no obligation to take part. Managers then told me who had agreed to take part so that I could contact them.

The research was conducted with two groups of social workers. First, I observed social workers in safeguarding teams who were engaged in the initial screening of referrals and assessments. Second, I interviewed social workers in adult community teams who carried out assessments and longer-term safeguarding work. The three participating local authority teams used different models to assess and manage safeguarding risks (these models are described in greater detail in Chapter 3).

I conducted research with 31 social workers in total: 17 were in safeguarding teams and 14 were in adult community teams. In terms of practice experience, interviewees ranged from team managers to newly qualified social workers doing their assessed and supported year in employment. All research participants were given pseudonyms. These are set out in Table 1 along with participants' gender, age and job role, and the local authority they were based in.

In each of the safeguarding teams, I shadowed a social worker for 4–6 hours. All social workers in the safeguarding teams were office based, so my observation consisted of sitting with them and observing how they conducted their work. This approach was suggested to me during an initial meeting with the safeguarding team in Fosborough; the team members thought that this would be the best way for me to understand what they were doing. I observed social workers who were on 'screening' that day, meaning that they were focusing on conducting safeguarding work and not

Table 1: Pseudonyms of social workers in safeguarding teams and adult community teams

Social workers in safeguarding teams

Pseudonym	Gender	Age band	Role	Local authority
Alice	Female	40–44	SW	Fosborough
Claire	Female	45–49	SP	Fosborough
Fiona	Female	30–34	SP	Fosborough
Candice	Female	45–49	SP	Fosborough
Lisa	Female	60–64	SP	Fosborough
Rebecca	Female	35–39	SP	Fosborough
Isobel	Female	30–34	SW	Fosborough
Amanda	Female	55–59	TM	Gainsborough
Mike	Male	50–54	SP	Gainsborough
Ram	Male	45–49	SP	Gainsborough
Nicola	Female	35–39	SP	Gainsborough
Penny	Female	35–39	SP	Gainsborough
Victoria	Female	30–34	SP	Gainsborough
Mavis	Female	60–64	SP	Almsbury
Kerry	Female	40–44	TM	Almsbury
Jenny	Female	55–59	SP	Almsbury

Social workers in adult community teams

Pseudonym	Gender	Age band	Role	Local authority
Hayley	Female	35–39	SP	Fosborough
Karen	Female	55–59	SP	Fosborough
Margaret	Female	50–54	TM	Fosborough
Nadia	Female	35–39	SP	Fosborough
Marcia	Female	40–44	TM	Fosborough
Rachel	Female	40–44	SP	Fosborough
Ingrid	Female	35–39	SW	Fosborough
Simon	Male	50–54	SW	Fosborough
Louise	Female	35–39	SW	Fosborough
Adrian	Male	35–39	SW	Fosborough
Faye	Female	45–49	SW	Gainsborough
Judith	Female	35–39	SW	Gainsborough
Patricia	Female	45–49	SW	Almsbury
Michelle	Female	40–44	SW	Almsbury
Sue	Female	30–34	SW	Almsbury

Note: SW stands for social worker, SP for senior practitioner and TM for team manager.

doing any other parts of their job. Typically, I sat next to the worker so that I could observe any data they were inputting into the computer system. As I was not familiar with how the computer systems worked, I asked social workers about the reasons for their actions. I asked open-ended questions to further understand their reasons. For example, if social workers indicated that policy, forms or computer systems influenced their practice, I then asked about how they used these, what their views on them were and how this affected their work.

During the research, I made regular field notes. Within ethnographic research, field notes typically provide a record of observations, jottings, ideas or emotional reactions to the research process (O'Reilly, 2012). Because note-taking is a common activity within social work, I was able to take notes without looking rude or distracted, and I could normally do so during periods when the worker was occupied. Typically, I would record key details about referral, the people involved and actions proposed in response to concerns. In line with suggestions by Spradley (2016b), I paid attention to the sequencing of events over time and the goals social workers were trying to achieve. I also attended to how objects, such as computer systems, affected the safeguarding process. Throughout the research, I aimed to be sensitive to the emotional reactions of the workers and my own emotional responses. At the end of the day, I conducted an interview with each safeguarding team social worker, in which I invited them to reflect on one of the cases I had observed. Social workers were asked to describe their thoughts and feelings on receiving the referral as well as how they decided on the aims of the work and what tasks needed to be completed and how they assessed identified risks. They were also invited to describe who they interviewed and how they assessed and managed risk. Finally, they were asked to identify organisational factors that helped or hindered their work. By focusing on particular cases in this way, my questions were less abstract, though I explained to the social workers that they were free to talk about other cases or safeguarding practice more generally if they wished.

I piloted observation of social workers in adult community teams, observing three social workers who were conducting longer-term safeguarding work. I did not go out on visits with any of these social workers, but observed them undertaking aspects of safeguarding work within the office, such as making calls to other professionals or documenting safeguarding work. Future attempts to observe such work were less successful, as most community-based social workers did not conduct their safeguarding work in one block, but conducted the work as and when they could. Consequently, I limited myself to interviews with the remaining social workers in adult community teams. These interviews followed a similar format to those with the social workers in safeguarding teams: I asked the participants to talk about a recent safeguarding case and then asked about how they conducted long-term safeguarding work.

However, with this group, I asked for their first thoughts on receiving the referral, what they saw as the main tasks to be completed and what the aims of the work were. I also asked them what their experiences of engaging with the referrer, service user, carers, professionals or other parties had been. The social workers were asked how they set out to assess the safeguarding risks, what they thought were the main risks to be managed (if any), and how they communicated those risks to others. They were also asked to reflect on what had gone well or badly, and whether they felt helped or hindered by their organisations.

I aimed to build rapport during interviews by adopting Spradley's (2016a) approach of starting with nonthreatening descriptive questions. Having established a rapport, I aimed to encourage participants to describe and expand on their experiences. I would generally ask what Kvale (1996) calls 'introducing questions' (for example, questions about their age and how long they had worked with safeguarding cases). I responded with nonverbal cues and verbal prompts (such as 'yes', 'ok' or 'right'). I also tended to paraphrase what the participant had said in the hope that this would prompt them to develop their ideas.

When using quotes in the book, I indicate whether they were drawn from my field notes or from interviews. The reason for this is that my field notes were completed during observations or slightly afterwards and so were limited by how fast I could write things down and by my memory. Interviews were recorded and transcribed, so the quotes used here are verbatim.

It is now well established that it is impossible for researchers to adopt a wholly neutral position when doing ethnographic research. To manage their own bias many researchers aim to be 'reflexive', meaning that they reflect regularly on how their own identity and background may affect the research process (Finlay, 2002). As part of this process, researchers may consider whether they are an 'insider', sharing a similar identity or status to the people they are researching, or an 'outsider'. As Dwyer and Buckle (2009) note, not all researchers fall into one camp or the other, and I saw myself as being in what these authors call 'the space between'. When inviting people to take part in the research, I explained that I was both a social worker and a social work academic. My identity as a social worker gave me 'insider status' in that the social workers I interviewed or observed were aware that I understood the values and language of social work. However, I also made it clear to participants that my own time as a practitioner had been spent in mental health teams. Additionally, social workers were aware that as a social work academic, I was primarily engaged in research and teaching rather than front-line practice. When doing the research, I observed that social workers reacted to me in different ways. As I presented myself as someone who had practice experience in mental health specifically, most social workers were willing to give me explanations of how safeguarding worked in their organisations without assuming too much prior knowledge on my part. However, my identity as an academic and researcher led some to concern that they were being tested. For example, one newly qualified social worker told me that she was very nervous about being observed, because I was "very clever" and she was just learning to do the job. To counter this tendency, I tried to reassure social workers that my aim was to observe differences in practice across social workers and authorities rather than assess whether they were doing safeguarding 'correctly'.

As someone with significant experience of front-line social work, I was aware that social work is never easy. My identity as a social worker, therefore, caused me some angst when analysing the data and writing up. This process has been described by Lisa Morriss, who is also a social work academic who has conducted ethnographic research. Reflecting on her feelings about sharing her findings with others, she writes:

> I used extracts from the interviews [from my research] during a talk at a neighbouring university. Speaking the words of the social workers out loud in a room full of mental health academics, service users and practitioners, I felt that, not only was I using their words to further my academic career, but also that I was betraying the social workers by opening them up to scrutiny by people they had never met. As a registered social worker, I felt extremely uncomfortable in allowing the social workers to be criticised by the room of 'strangers'. (Morriss, 2016b, p 534)

As I wrote my account, I had similar worries about how my research might be perceived. While my intention is to understand cultures of practice, I am aware that such accounts might be used to criticise front-line practitioners. While this risk can never be completely removed, my intention is to allow social workers, practitioners and academics to understand how risk is managed within adult safeguarding. Through my research, I hope to identify the strengths and limitations of current practices and identify ways in which things might be done differently.

The structure of the book

The first chapter of the book is called 'The problem of adult safeguarding'. In this, I examine how adult abuse and neglect in England came to be seen as a problem needing a policy response. Drawing on social policy literature, I show how social problems have been conceptualised (Blumer, 1971; Best, 2013). I then give a history of policy responses to adult abuse and neglect. The chapter explores campaigns led by Barbara Robb against the abuse and neglect of older people in National Health Service (NHS) hospitals in the

1960s, before setting out the concerns about elder abuse that were prevalent in the 1970s. I then cover the re-emergence of concerns about elder abuse as well as concerns about the abuse of people with learning disabilities in the 1980s. After this, I focus on the development of early guidance in the 1990s and the publication of *No Secrets: Guidance on Developing and Implementing Multi-agency Policies and Procedures to Protect Vulnerable Adults from Abuse* (Department of Health, 2000) and subsequent debates about safeguarding in the 2000s. I also describe the various scandals which led to the introduction of the Care Act 2014, which made adult safeguarding a statutory duty for the first time. In the remainder of the chapter, I focus on the reception to safeguarding duties under the Care Act 2014 and highlight the issue of rising referral rates.

In the second chapter of the book, 'Risk and social work', I introduce the topic of risk and uncertainty to readers. Drawing on the sociology of risk and uncertainty, I set out three ways of thinking about risk. I begin by outlining Ulrich Beck's theory of risk society, then explore Mary Douglas' ideas on risk and culture, followed by theories of governmentality as set out by Michel Foucault and expanded by others. I present these theories to provide readers who are new to the sociology of risk with a basic understanding of the key theories. Having done this, I turn to social work perspectives on risk. Here, I identify how social work academics have applied risk theory to social policy and social work, and consider relevant research findings. I set out what I think are the limitations of current social work theory and identify how I think social work can learn from new theoretical perspectives on 'risk work' which pay closer attention to how risk is assessed and managed on the ground.

In the next three chapters of the book, I report on my research findings. The title of Chapter 3 is 'Referrals and assessments'. Local authorities are faced with rising numbers of referrals: statistics from NHS Digital (2022) show sharp increases since 2016. I explore how social workers in safeguarding teams screened assessments, describing the technical processes they went through and considering their reasons for rejecting certain referrals. I also look at social workers' views on the external factors shaping their work, such as national or local policies, findings from safeguarding inquiries and austerity.

In Chapter 4, 'Personalised safeguarding: policy, principles and practice realities', I focus on some of the tensions between policy and practice. I begin by looking at how the social workers in my study perceived policy initiatives designed to make adult safeguarding focus on the wishes of service users. I then look at some of the tensions within practice, namely the impact of austerity and decreasing resources in local authorities. I also focus on social workers' interpretation of the principle of wellbeing and the safeguarding principles within the *Care and Support Statutory Guidance* (DHSC, 2022).

The title of Chapter 5 is 'Doing adult safeguarding with service users and carers'. In this chapter, I focus on how social workers conducted risk work with service users as well as with family carers and care agencies who were providing home care or care within care or nursing homes. I begin by considering how risk assessments were used within local authorities. Then, I explore the practical problems social workers raised in relation to person-led and outcome-focused social work, and I set out the steps social workers took when engaging with people around their safeguarding risks. In the remainder of the chapter, I focus on how social workers engaged with family carers and social care agencies, looking at the steps taken to establish trust as well as at how professional power was used.

In the final chapter, 'Conclusion', I bring the findings of the previous chapters together. Returning to the sociology of risk and uncertainty, I reflect on what social work practice in adult safeguarding tells us about the nature of risk work. I also lay out the policy and practice implications and suggest what the next steps for adult safeguarding in England might be. But before we get there, let's consider how adult safeguarding came to be seen as a policy issue in the first place.

1

The problem of adult safeguarding

Introduction

I qualified to be a social worker in England in 1998. During my time in training, nobody used the term 'adult safeguarding'. The concept, as it is understood now, did not exist. This situation is very different from where we find ourselves today. Adult safeguarding is now seen as a central part of social work practice in England. The Care Act 2014 sets out the legal duties of local authorities, and social workers are often acutely aware of the law and policy. Adult safeguarding training is a core part of the social work curriculum. Also, there is increased public understanding of adult abuse and neglect (Yoeli et al, 2016). In the present day, it can be hard to understand why adult safeguarding was not seen as important for so long. And the ever-rising rate of adult safeguarding referrals and enquiries seems to attest to the fact that it is a problem of some scale (NHS Digital, 2022). This raises the question of how we got here and how safeguarding came to be understood in its current form.

In this chapter, I consider how adult safeguarding has come to be viewed as an issue needing a policy response. Adult safeguarding or adult protection systems have evolved in several countries, including England, Wales, Scotland, Ireland, Canada and Australia (Donnelly et al, 2017) although here I limit myself to an analysis of the situation in England. While others have examined how adult safeguarding policy has evolved in relation to care homes and hospitals (Manthorpe and Stevens, 2015), my analysis is broader in range, focusing on all aspects of adult safeguarding. I begin by setting out a history which highlights how policy has developed, identifying campaigns, public inquiries, political discussion and policy developments from the 1960s to the Care Act 2014 and beyond.

Abuse and neglect exist in all societies and are sometimes referred to as being 'as old as time itself'. However, as Blumer (1971) states, some harms are identified as social problems, while others are not. Because of this, we need to understand how particular issues within society come to be seen as problems in need of policy response. In this chapter, I adopt what is known as a social constructionist position, meaning that I focus on how meaning and knowledge about adult safeguarding have evolved. To provide some structure for the first part of my chapter, I set out what Best (2013) (drawing on Blumer, 1971) describes as a 'natural history' of social problems.

According to Best (2013), social problems go through six stages. First, 'people make claims that there is a social problem, with certain characteristics, causes and solutions' (Best, 2013, p 19). Claims may be made by activists or by experts, who are referred to as 'claims-makers'. Second, the issue may gain media coverage. Here, claims-makers may seek press coverage to alert the public to the issue and to exert pressure on policy makers. Third, claims may lead to a public reaction where members of the public learn about a claim and form opinions about it. Fourth, policymaking takes place, with policies or laws being created by government to address the claims that have been raised. Fifth, state agencies engage in social problem work to implement these policies. In the sixth and final stage, different parties respond to policy outcomes. This may involve individuals pointing out the shortcomings of current arrangements and proposing change. When examining these claims, it is important to consider the resources that claims-makers have, such as money, status or power, as those with more power are more likely to get their views heard. We also need to consider the rhetoric which claims-makers use. In other words, what kinds of language or argument are used to describe the issue and persuade people that it is problematic?

The history I present in this chapter draws on library research and analysis of policy documents. I show that what we have come to understand as adult safeguarding has emerged as the result of multiple claims by different groups of people. I begin my history in the 1960s, focusing on concerns raised about the treatment of people with mental health problems who had been placed in psychiatric hospitals.

The 1960s: Barbara Robb's campaign

This history begins with an examination the abuse and neglect of older people in long-stay hospitals. Public attention was drawn to the issue through the book *Sans Everything: A Case to Answer* (Robb, 1967). The book became a bestseller (Hilton, 2017b) and consisted of chapters by hospital visitors, nurses and social workers which described the degrading treatment of older adults in seven hospitals. *Sans Everything* was part of a wider campaign to draw attention to the mistreatment of adults in hospital, led by Barbara Robb, a psychotherapist by profession.

Barbara Robb first became aware of the mistreatment of older people in 1965 when visiting Amy Gibbs, a patient who had been admitted to Friern Hospital, a psychiatric unit in London. Amy's deterioration since her admission in 1963 and the conditions at Friern shocked Robb, leading her to document them in a diary (Hilton, 2017a). Robb was particularly concerned by a practice known as 'stripping', which was common in 1960s long-stay hospitals. This involved removing patient's personal possessions, including their glasses, dentures and hearing aids, on the basis that it was easier to treat passive patients than active ones (Hilton, 2017a). Robb's conversations with Amy and the relatives of other patients highlighted a range of accusations, such as nurses hitting patients for being incontinent, threatening them and taunting them. Furthermore, Amy was frightened about complaining about the treatment, telling Robb that the nurses had threatened to put her 'out into the street' (Robb, 1967, pp 82–3).

Robb had more power than the typical activist, being friends with several influential members of society, such as Lord and Lady Strabolgi and Audrey Harvey, a citizens' rights campaigner. Robb kept a diary of events, which she asked other visitors to corroborate. This was sent to Minister of Health Kenneth Robinson, via Lord Strabolgi, who also made suggestions about how care might be improved and gave a speech in the House of Lords (Hansard, 1965). Following this, the Ministry of Health arranged for Robb to meet the head of mental health at the ministry, Dr Geoffrey Tooth. However, Robb was disappointed to find that the issues had not been investigated, with Tooth advising her not to raise a complaint in case 'something brutal' occurred to Amy (Hilton, 2017a, p 81).

Robb's dismissal by the head of mental health led her to engage in activism by forming Aid for the Elderly in Government Institutions (AEGIS) in October 1965 (Hilton, 2017a). One of AEGIS' first activities was to submit a letter to *The Times* newspaper, signed by several lords, bishops and professors. The letter highlighted the practice of stripping, alleged that the Ministry of Health mishandled complaints and called on others to come forward with further examples of poor care or mistreatment. Robb then published *Sans Everything* (1967), documenting Amy Gibbs' mistreatment and also giving evidence of abuse in other hospitals.

Accusations in *Sans Everything* and the *News of the World* newspaper prompted the government to act by commissioning seven hospital inquiries (Hilton, 2017a), though the regional hospital boards were allowed to appoint their own inquiry committees. The reports from these inquiries adopted a 'doctor knows best' mentality, writing off complainants as uneducated or simple-minded and attributing poor care to a few 'bad apples' (Butler and Drakeford, 2003, p 37). The Minister for Health concluded that the allegations in *Sans Everything* were 'totally unfounded or grossly exaggerated' (cited in Hilton, 2017a, p 208). This response backfired, being viewed as a whitewash by the press and increasing public support for AEGIS.

Following the ongoing press attention on the treatment of older adults in hospitals, Minister for Health and Social Security Richard Crossman adopted a different approach, ordering a full inquiry into the conditions at Ely Hospital, a large institution for people with learning disabilities (Fyson et al, 2004). This was chaired by Geoffrey Howe, QC. Howe's inquiry noted that care within the hospital was 'old fashioned, unduly rough and

[of] undesirably low standards' (Department of Health and Social Security, 1973, p 24), that staff who complained were victimised and that leadership was poor. However, as Butler and Drakeford (2003) note, much of the mistreatment was seen as the result of unsophisticated nursing techniques. Statements by a key whistle-blower, which later became available through the Public Record Office, presented a starker picture of violence. One excerpt notes that:

> In Ward 23, there is a charge nurse named John Edwards who everyone considers to be a sadist. He has an assistant named Kay who falls into the same category. A young patient named Kevin is constantly going into the kitchen which is out of bounds. He is regularly beaten by the two nurses. On one occasion Edwards took him to his office and beat him. I heard the screams. (Cited in Butler and Drakeford, 2003, p 50)

The findings of the inquiry were embarrassing for the Labour Government, leading it to launch the Hospital Advisory Service (Hilton, 2017a). This organisation was independent from the Department of Health, though clinically led, and examined the service offered by hospitals (although it did not examine individual complaints). Actions by AEGIS also contributed to the development of an NHS ombudsman, which encouraged the NHS to develop more transparent complaints procedures.

In summary, several points can be noted about claims of adult abuse in this period. For a claim to be effective, claims-makers had to put forward a persuasive argument. These claims may consist of grounds (information and evidence about the condition), warrants (appeals to values) and conclusions (recommendations for future policy or practice; Best, 2013). AEGIS' claims appealed to the new public values emerging in the 1960s, namely autonomy and public ownership of the NHS (Hilton, 2017a). While ministers initially tried to discredit AEGIS' claims, continuing press coverage and fear of what the public might think drove the Ely Hospital inquiry, leading to the establishment of the Hospital Advisory Service and a revised system for hospital complaints.

The 1970s: early concerns about 'granny battering'

The beginning of the 1970s saw a change of government, with the Conservative Party defeating Labour. Once in power, the government commissioned a committee to review the hospital complaints system (Hilton, 2017a). The committee identified that further reform was needed, and this led to a 26-point code focusing on how complaints should be managed. Following these changes, the issue of abuse in hospitals fell off the political agenda and was gaining little public or press attention.

The 1970s did, however, see the emerge of claims about the abuse of older people in the community, initially described as 'granny battering' or 'granny bashing'. These concerns need to be seen in context of the coverage about child abuse and 'baby battering' that was prevalent at that time. Medical concerns about 'battered baby syndrome' arose in the 1960s but came to public attention through the Maria Colwell inquiry (Parton, 1979). Maria Colwell, at 7 years old, was killed by her stepfather after being returned home following a period in foster care. The case attracted much press attention, and this was instrumental in child abuse becoming recognised as a social problem (Parton, 1979). While adult abuse did not receive the same degree of attention in the press, psychiatrists began to speak about it in professional publications in the United Kingdom (Burston, 1975; Baker, 1981). These concerns are neatly encapsulated in a letter by B.J. Burston, a psychiatrist, to the *British Medical Journal*:

> Sir,—Hardly a week goes by without some reference in the national press or medical journals to baby-battering, and I think it is about time that all of us realized that elderly people too are at times deliberately battered. I have personal knowledge of cases in which it has been possible to confirm that elderly patients have been battered by relatives before admission to hospital and in which there has been no doubt that the battering was deliberate. In other cases assault at home has been suspected but could not be confirmed. This leads one to wonder how many of the elderly who 'fall down frequently, doctor' do so because they are assaulted. [...] Perhaps general practitioners in particular and casualty officers especially should become as conscious of granny-battering as they are now aware of baby-battering. Community nurses, health visitors, and social workers should also have this aspect of 'caring for the elderly' drawn to their attention. (Burston, 1975, p 592)

Psychiatrists hypothesised that several factors might account for 'granny battering', including the higher rates of abuse in society more generally, the ageing population and the lack of support for those who experienced abuse (Walshe-Brennan, 1977; Baker, 1981). Drawing on the accounts of nurses, Walshe-Brennan (1977) suggested that the problem was worsening and that doctors tended to disbelieve reports of abuse. However, coverage in UK medical journals fizzled out (until the 1990s).

Claims-makers seek to draw attention to an issue by adopting the language of other social problems to 'piggyback' onto existing concerns (Best, 2013). Use of the term 'granny bashing' was a clear attempt to align adult abuse with child abuse and to argue that both should receive professional attention. While references to these letters and articles are frequently cited in histories of adult abuse, they had very little impact in the press or on public perceptions, being limited to academic or clinical journals, which few people read. However, the 1980s would see the emergence of new claims-makers who would be more successful in raising concern about the issue.

The 1980s: concerns about old-age abuse and the abuse of people with learning disabilities

The early 1980s saw the issue of 'granny battering' picked up by Mervyn Eastman, a practising social worker in London (see Eastman, 1980, 1982; Eastman and Sutton, 1982). His first article, 'The battering of Mrs. Scarfe', published in *New Age* defined 'granny battering' as 'the systematic physical abuse of an elderly person by a relative' (cited in McCreadie, 1993, p 8). Eastman noted a lack of research in this area, which he saw as discouraging professionals from recognising the issue. Nonetheless, he set out a series of signposts which might indicate the possibility of abuse having taken place. These included dependence on a relative, poor family communication, history of repeated falls, bruising and cramped housing conditions. Perhaps more unusual for the modern reader, the issue of 'role reversal' was set out as a warning sign. This was seen to occur in cases where a person who had been cared for by the older adult was now caring for them, leading to resentment on the part of the carer. Later articles by Eastman expanded the definition by noting that abuse could be physical, emotional, psychological (Eastman and Sutton, 1982) or sexual (Eastman, 1982). Eastman later wrote that the term 'granny battering' was disparaging, and his book reframed the problem as 'old age abuse' (Eastman, 1984).

While calls by Eastman for more attention to the issue were ignored by government, Age Concern England (now Age UK) became concerned and commissioned a review of research (see McCreadie, 1993). This highlighted that there was no agreed definition of abuse, that most research studies on the issue were small in scale and that the current levels of abuse and its causes remained unknown. Age Concern England published Eastman's book *Old Age Abuse* (1984) and established a consultative group to review the law in relation to 'vulnerable elderly people' (Greengross, 1986). The charity argued that current laws were scattered and ill-used. This was because workers had a low level of awareness about existing laws, but also because the laws were unwieldly or difficult to apply to the cases that practitioners had experience with. The group considered establishment of specific powers, including the duty to consider the case of a vulnerable adult or their carer, and also argued that there should be greater public awareness of elder abuse and clearer referral procedures. A multidisciplinary conference was held by the British Geriatrics Society in 1989, and this highlighted growing academic interest in the issue (Tomlin, 1989).

The 1980s also saw concerns arise about the abuse and neglect of people with learning disabilities. The context of this concern was community care policies, through which people who had been housed in long-stay hospitals were moved into supported or independent housing. These policies were first introduced in the 1960s, but had stalled due to the lack of coordination between health trusts and local authorities (Bartlett and Sandland, 2014). The Conservative Government sought to revive community care policies (see Department of Health, 1989), with 'normalisation' or 'normal life' philosophies being promoted (Alaszewski, 1999). Such policies held that individuals should be empowered to gain control over their lives through being given the right to engage in jobs or relationships. While few commentators doubted normalisation policies were a good thing, concerns were expressed about the vulnerability of people with learning disabilities. For example, a paper published in 1987 by Hewitt, a police officer, expressed worry about how those with learning disabilities would fare in the community. He wrote:

> people with mental handicaps are very vulnerable. They are very trusting, mostly quite honest and have a love some might envy. What is so odious, is that those in positions which give them advantage will sometimes abuse it. There must be justice and we can all do something to see that it is upheld. (Hewitt, 1987, p 131)

Although Hewitt's characterisation of people with learning disabilities seems clumsy now, he highlighted several worries which were echoed by others. Studies in the late 1980s highlighted that people with learning disabilities were being victimised in community homes (Williams, 1993), and Hewitt's concerns reflected growing worries among the public and professionals that such issues were being ignored. The case of Beverley Lewis brought these worries into focus. Beverley was a young deaf-blind Black woman with learning and physical disabilities who lived with her mother. In February 1989, she was found dead on the family sofa, weighing just four stone and wrapped in newspaper. Press reports noted that access to Beverley had been refused repeatedly by her mother, who had mental health problems (Simcock and Manthorpe, 2014). The inquest reported death by natural causes and no agencies were blamed. However, the family went on to make their dissatisfaction with the inquest known. In national television and radio interviews, they blamed the social worker leading the case and identified poor communication between agencies (Simcock and Manthorpe, 2014). These issues would be picked up by activists and politicians in the 1990s.

In summary, the 1980s saw a greater number of claims being made about adult abuse than had been the case in the 1970s. What is notable about this decade is that a wider range of claims-makers emerged. Claims were initiated by 'experts', in the form of social workers and police officers voicing concerns from practice. Claims about elder abuse gained the backing of national charities, providing a larger platform. Press coverage of the abuse of Beverley Lewis also brought the issue of adult abuse to public attention, a pattern which would be repeated with inquiries in the next decade.

The 1990s: early guidance and the Law Commission reviews

The beginning of the 1990s saw the introduction of the National Health Service and Community Care Act 1990, passed by the Conservative Government under Margaret Thatcher. The Act, which received royal assent on 29 June 1990, was significant for making a split between purchasers and providers, for creating an internal market within the NHS and for changing local authority functions. However, it provided little provision for defining, assessing or managing abuse and neglect. Section 47 gave local authorities a duty to conduct an assessment where they became aware that a person needed services due to actual or potential abuse or neglect, but gave little direction beyond this.

Although the National Health Service and Community Care Act 1990 made little provision for adult abuse, the Department of Health did commission a review of research evidence (McCreadie, 1991). This supported the message that little was known about the context or prevalence of adult abuse. However, research by the Social Services Inspectorate the following year looked at levels of abuse within two local authorities (Sutton, 1992). Within this study, 64 cases of elder abuse were identified by social workers, including physical, psychological and financial abuse. Professional responses were viewed as uncoordinated, with workers unsure how to proceed. In addition, academic research began to emerge which highlighted the scale of elder abuse. A survey of adults aged 60 and over in Great Britain asked participants whether they had been abused by a family member or relative (Ogg and Bennett, 1992). It found that 5 per cent of older adults reported psychological abuse, 2 per cent reported physical abuse and 2 per cent reported financial abuse.

Growing awareness of adult abuse led professionals to come together to campaign on the issue. In 1993, the pressure group Action on Elder Abuse (now Hourglass) was formed. Supported by Age Concern England, its mission was to 'prevent abuse in old age by promoting changes in policy and practice through raising awareness, education, promoting research and the collection and dissemination of such information' (cited in Penhale and Kingston, 1995, p 225). Concern about the issue of adult abuse spread beyond professionals, and family groups began to lobby on the issue. For example, Voice UK, formed by parents who discovered that their daughter had been raped by a member of staff while in residential care, aimed to effect change through highlighting examples of bad practice and advocating for changes to the legal system (Horrocks, 2000).

Also in 1993, two documents were published aiming to address adult abuse, but these lacked bite. First, the Social Services Inspectorate issued professional guidance in the form of *No Longer Afraid: The Safeguard of Older People in Domestic Settings* (Department of Health and Social Services Inspectorate, 1993). The definition of abuse given in the document built on previous ones by acknowledging that abuse could be temporary as well as systematic. However, as workers had no statutory powers to manage elder abuse, they were forced to address it through existing assessment and care management procedures (Biggs, 1996). The second document came out of a two-day workshop funded by the NHS and the Social Services Inspectorate and hosted by the Association for Residential Care (ARC) and the National Association for the Protection from Sexual Abuse of Adults and Children with Learning Disabilities (NAPSAC). The workshop covered the issue of sexual abuse of people with learning disabilities. This led to practice guidance suggesting how sexual abuse should be tackled in residential care settings (ARC and NAPSAC, 1993). However, the guidance was published by ARC and NAPSAC rather than by the government, leading critics to question whether local authorities would act on their suggestions (Hardiker, 1994).

Following an internal inquiry into the Beverley Lewis case by Gloucester Social Services, the pressure group Sense (a group supporting people with complex disabilities) called for a public inquiry into the case (Simcock and Manthorpe, 2014). This call was rejected by the Parliamentary Under-Secretary for Health, Stephen Dorrell (Hansard, 1990). However, the government did ask the Law Commission[1] to consider and advise on the coroner's view that law in this area should be clarified. The Law Commission's (1995) report on mental incapacity expressed growing concerns about elder abuse and the abuse of disabled people. It noted that many organisations had identified the need for legal powers to deal with crisis situations. It stated:

> To the basic question of whether any reform of these emergency powers was needed our consultees responded with a resounding affirmative. The existing law[2] was said to be ineffective in protecting elderly, disabled and other vulnerable people from abuse and neglect, and inadequate in its approach to issues of autonomy and individual rights. It appeared to be counter-productive, being so draconian that it was rarely used. (Law Commission, 1995, para 9.1)

Its final report on mental incapacity (Law Commission, 1995) also expressed concern about 'vulnerable people'. It proposed that local authorities should be given new powers to investigate abuse and neglect of vulnerable adults. It also recommended that local authorities should be given short-term powers to assess whether a person was at risk and, where professionals were obstructed, powers to enter and remove the person.

At the time of this review, several independent inquiries made the issue of adult abuse more visible. In 1996, the Beech House inquiry drew attention to the issue of elder abuse in hospitals, focusing on the systemic abuse of 13 older adults with mental health problems at Beech House in London (Camden and Islington Community Health Services NHS Trust, 1999). The inquiry found that staff had punched and slapped patients, given them cold baths and restrained them inappropriately. It also highlighted poor clinical standards, acceptance of ulcers and pressure sores, unauthorised absences from the ward by staff and dishonest record-keeping. The Longcare inquiry (Buckinghamshire County Council, 1998) received even broader coverage due to the number of people involved and the protracted period over which it was undertaken (Stanley and Manthorpe, 2004). It focused on abuse against people with learning disabilities in two residential homes owned and managed by Gordon Rowe, an ex-social worker. While the inquiry report was discrete about the details of the abuse, press reports revealed that residents had been indecently assaulted, raped, injured with scissors and made to lie on cold, wet grass as a punishment (Smith and Clement, 2003; Fyson et al, 2004). The resulting press scandal led to questions in Parliament with Paul Boateng (then Parliamentary Under Secretary of State for Disabled People) stating:

> We take the issue of abuse very seriously. We are determined to send a clear and unambiguous message that abuse in residential care will not be tolerated. The promulgation of good practice based on respect for the individual, and the importance of being able to identify and remedy actual or potential abuse, is a vital part of the Department's funding strategy, as is its work on developing a credible and comprehensive regulatory framework based on national regulatory standards. (Hansard, 1997)

The government's response to the Law Commission report suggested that it was edging toward giving professionals powers to address adult abuse and neglect (Lord Chancellor, 1997). It accepted its recommendations on creating new compulsory powers and sought views on their practicalities. However, following the consultation, the government decided not to proceed. No reasons for this decision were given (see Joint Committee on the Draft Mental Incapacity Bill, 2003).

The 1990s saw greater recognition of the issue of adult abuse. While the National Health Service and Community Care Act 1990 had failed to address the issue, the decade saw an increase in claims-makers highlighting adult abuse as a social problem. As in the 1980s, many of these claims were made by welfare professionals. However, the number of groups campaigning on the issue was starting to grow, with professionals and family carers becoming more organised and public inquiries making the issue more visible. While we can't be sure how the public reacted to these reports, concerns about abuse were beginning to filter down to policy makers. While the government was resistant to providing professionals with legal powers to respond to adult abuse, the 2000s would see significant steps taken to address the issue within policy.

The 2000s: publication of *No Secrets* and debates on the future of safeguarding

The beginning of the 2000s saw the government following up on policy from the 1990s. First, the government introduced new measures to regulate residential care settings outside of the NHS. National minimum standards were introduced under the Care Standards Act 2000, which came into effect in July of that year. Second, *No Secrets: Guidance on Developing and Implementing Multi-agency Policies and Procedures to Protect Vulnerable Adults from Abuse* (Department of Health, 2000) was published. This guidance was significant in outlining a national approach to adult protection, providing guidance to social services departments (who were identified as 'lead agency'), NHS trusts, health authorities and the police. Agencies were instructed to collaborate closely on developing local codes of practice and to take steps to prevent abuse from occurring. The document defined abuse in relation to 'vulnerable adults' as 'a violation of an individual's human and civil rights by any other person or persons' (Department of Health, 2000, para 2.5). This definition included acts of both commission and omission, covering physical, sexual, psychological and financial abuse, neglect and discrimination.

Following the publication of *No Secrets* (Department of Health, 2000), local authorities set to work at putting the policy in place. Research studies found that local authorities and other agencies adopted the definitions of abuse given in *No Secrets* and most had multi-agency procedures in place by 2001 (Sumner, 2002; Filinson, 2007). However, several problems were evident. Local authorities reported that they did not have the resources to apply *No Secrets* effectively (Mathew et al, 2002). Survey research by the Practitioner Alliance against Abuse of Vulnerable Adults also found that key areas of practice within the guidance were not being consistently addressed (Filinson, 2007).[3]

In 2002–03, the issue of adult abuse received parliamentary attention once more when the Joint Committee on the Draft Mental Capacity Bill (2003) reviewed the proposed legislation. The report was critical of the progress made through *No Secrets* (Department of Health, 2000) and cited evidence from witnesses to support this. In the report, Graham Collingridge from the Association of Directors of Social Services (ADSS) stated that the government had provided no extra resources when implementing the guidance and noted wide variations in practice across local authorities. Also a leading judge, Master Lush, representing the Court of Protection, stated that the police were reluctant to become involved in adult abuse cases. And John Williams, a professor of law, said that social workers and health professionals were frustrated by a lack of power to intervene, even where they were aware that abuse was taking place. He opined that existing policy, 'tolerates financial abuse, tolerates physical abuse, and basically there is nothing that can be done' (Joint Committee on the Draft Mental Incapacity Bill, 2003, para 259). In response to these concerns, the Joint Committee recommended that, 'statutory authorities should be given additional powers of investigation and intervention in cases of alleged physical, sexual or financial abuse of people lacking the capacity to protect themselves from the risk of abuse' (2003, para 266).

In its response to the Scrutiny Committee of the Mental Capacity Bill, the government resisted calls to introduce new safeguarding powers (Department for Constitutional Affairs, 2004). They argued that the *No Secrets* guidance (Department of Health, 2000) already required local authorities to liaise with other agencies to protect vulnerable adults. They also stated that adult protection should not be addressed under mental incapacity legislation, because 'it is right that this [*No Secrets* guidance] extends beyond adults who lack capacity to all vulnerable adults' (Department for Constitutional Affairs, 2004, para 15). New legal powers were viewed as unnecessary on the grounds that Section 47 of the National Assistance Act 1948 already provided a duty to investigate and gave compulsory powers. In making this argument, the government ignored the arguments by the Law Commission (1995) that these powers were unsuitable in most cases and rarely used in practice.

The issue of adult abuse also received government attention in 2003–04 with the report of the House of Commons Health Committee on Elder Abuse (2004). The report opened with evidence from Gary Fitzgerald, Chief Executive of Action on Elder Abuse. This read:

> Mr Fitzgerald pointed out that many people would be familiar with case of Victoria Climbié, a child tortured and murdered in the care of a relative, but that few knew about Margaret Panting, a 78-year-old woman from Sheffield who died after suffering 'unbelievable cruelty' while living with relatives. After her death in 2001, a post-mortem found 49 injuries on her body including cuts probably made by a razor blade and cigarette burns. (House of Commons Health Committee on Elder Abuse, 2004, para 1)

The committee made a wide range of recommendations to address elder abuse. These included broadening the definition of abuse to include those who did not receive support services, multidisciplinary research to establish the scale of abuse, training to enable workers to recognise abuse, better regulation of care staff and better advocacy services. The government responded by highlighting initiatives it had already implemented, namely the Modernisation of Adult Social Services Research initiative to improve data collection on elder abuse; the Care Standards Act 2000, The Care Homes Regulations 2001 and the Domiciliary Care Agencies Regulations 2002 (HM Government, 2004).

Despite the government's reluctance to introduce new measures, several bills were coming into legal effect which would have an impact on the prevention and management of adult abuse. The Mental Capacity Act 2005, implemented in 2007, was relevant in three respects (Filinson, 2007). First, it was established that a person should not be treated as unable to make a decision merely because they make an unwise decision. Where individuals were judged to lack capacity, professionals were instructed to act in their best interests, meaning that neglect should be addressed. Second, the Act established the Office of the Public Guardian. This promoted the use of lasting powers of attorney and enduring powers of attorney, which encouraged individuals to state who should act on their behalf should they lose capacity. In promoting these provisions, the government hoped that cases of financial abuse would be reduced. Third, Section 44 of the Act made the ill treatment or wilful neglect of a person who lacked capacity an offence – a power designed to prevent abuse.

Existing law and guidance on managing adult abuse was supplemented in 2005 by *Safeguarding Adults: A National Framework of Standards for Good Practice and Outcomes in Adult Protection Work*, published by the ADSS (2005). The ADSS had recognised in 2004 that the *No Secrets* guidance (Department of Health, 2000) needed further development, and it developed a series of good practice standards in conjunction with government departments, intended to be used as an audit tool. The guidance was notable for introducing the term 'safeguarding adults' in preference to 'vulnerable adults', which was used previously (Law Commission, 1995; Department of Health, 2000). Several arguments were made in favour of this. First, the term 'vulnerable adults' could be misinterpreted, as it focuses on vulnerability of the person experiencing abuse rather than focusing on the perpetrator of abuse. Second, the criteria which had been adopted in the government's Fair Access to Care Services criteria (DHSC (Department of Health and Social Care), 2002) focused on 'risk to independence and wellbeing' as the key criteria for eligibility, making the concept of vulnerable adult redundant. Third, policy now enabled adults to access care of their own choosing. In recognition of these changes, safeguarding adults was defined as 'all work which enables an adult "who is or may be eligible for community care services" to retain independence, wellbeing and choice and to access their human right to live a life that is free from abuse and neglect' (ADSS, 2005, p 5). This shift in language appeared to be widely accepted by those in the sector, with a later government consultation finding that 90 per cent of respondents favoured the phrase 'adult at risk' (Department of Health, 2008b).

The newly named ADASS continued to campaign for the improvement of adult safeguarding, arranging a series of workshops in 2007 with the Commission for Social Care Inspection, which lobbied for further legal powers to be introduced (Johnson, 2008). The demands of ADASS had been prompted by new research into adult abuse, funded by Comic Relief and the Department of Health (Johnson, 2008). The research was the first nationally representative study of elder abuse in the UK (O'Keeffe et al, 2007). The study sampled 2,100 people living in private households aged 66 and over. It found that 2.6 per cent of respondents in private households (including sheltered housing) reported that they had experienced mistreatment from a family, friend or care worker in the last year. When a broader measure of mistreatment was used, which included neighbours and close acquaintances, the level of mistreatment was 4 per cent. Types of mistreatment reported included neglect (1.1 per cent), financial abuse (0.7 per cent), psychological abuse (0.4 per cent), physical abuse (0.4 per cent) and sexual abuse (0.2 per cent). Care homes and hospitals were excluded, and the study was unable to access people affected by dementia.

Following the publication of the national study on elder abuse (O'Keeffe et al, 2007), the Minister for Care Services, Ivan Lewis, announced a review of *No Secrets*. In the consultation document, the government claimed that there were three reasons for holding the review (Department of Health, 2008a). First, it was important to establish whether *No Secrets* was appropriate for the current policy environment. Personalisation, which had been introduced with the aim of increasing self-assessment and management and providing eligible people with direct payments through which they could purchase their own care (HM Government, 2007), topped this list. Second, the report noted that stakeholders and researchers had reported deficiencies in the existing safeguarding system. Specifically, it was noted that implementation had been slow and inconsistent, that joint working was patchy and that some partners had been unwilling to 'come to the table' (Department of Health, 2008a, p 6). Third, they conceded that there had been calls for new statutory powers and that there was a need to examine the case for legislative change. Looking at responses to the consultation, 60 per cent of respondents supported new powers to enter a premises where there were suspicions that a vulnerable adult was being abused, although only 22 per cent felt that this should apply where an individual had mental capacity (Spencer-Lane, 2014).

In summary, the period of 2000–09 saw a high degree of activity in relation to debates around adult abuse or safeguarding. These debates followed on from concerns in the 1990s, with the government issuing guidance on protecting vulnerable adults through *No Secrets* (Department of Health, 2000). This guidance had set national standards, accelerating procedures already in place in some local authorities. However, implementation was uneven across the country. The report of the Joint Committee on the Draft Mental Capacity Bill (2003) and the report of the House of Commons Health Committee on Elder Abuse (2004) provided two high-profile forums in which the problem of adult abuse could be debated, and a range of claims-makers appeared before both. These individuals and organisations were largely united in their view that not enough was being done to address abuse and that further legal powers were needed. While the government initially resisted these claims, the findings of the national study on elder abuse (O'Keeffe et al, 2007) prompted them to revise their position, leading to national consultation (Department of Health, 2008a, 2008b) which would inform the Care Act 2014 in the next decade.

2010 and beyond: high-profile scandals, the Care Act 2014 and after

In 2010, the Department of Health and the Welsh Assembly Government agreed to review the adult social care system, and the Law Commission was tasked with reviewing the legal frameworks (see Law Commission, 2010). Formal efforts to shape safeguarding responses came about as part of that review, which took place over a three-year period. Safeguarding practice was also influenced by the LGA, the ADASS and the Social Care Institute for Excellence, who promoted the Making Safeguarding Personal initiative throughout the decade. The first Making Safeguarding Personal toolkit was published in 2010 (Ogilvie and Williams, 2010) with the aim of aligning safeguarding with other adult care initiatives, most notably personalisation, and ensuring that people experiencing a safeguarding enquiry were given choice about how their case was being managed (see Redley et al, 2015).

McAdam (2000) argues that at certain points in time, cultural opportunities arise in which the public becomes more willing to listen to claims-making. While the problem of adult abuse had been discussed within government committees in the 1990s and some adult abuse cases had received press attention, the level of coverage had been limited. Press coverage of the public inquiry into the Mid Staffordshire NHS Foundation Trust would be of a new order, receiving regular attention in 2010–14 (BBC, 2014). Mistreatment at this hospital came to light due to high mortality figures, discovered by the Healthcare Commission (now the Care Quality Commission – CQC) and due to campaigning by the pressure group Cure the NHS (Holmes, 2013).

The founder of Cure the NHS was Julie Bailey, whose mother had died at Stafford Hospital. Bailey recalled that she and her family had become aware that Stafford Hospital was unsafe when her mother was admitted there in 2007, their concern being so high that they had refused to leave her side. Following her mother's death, Bailey made complaints to the hospital's chief executive and director of nursing and to her local MP. Finding her concerns dismissed, she wrote a letter of appeal to the *Staffordshire Post* asking if other families had witnessed similar treatment. In an interview in 2009, she stated:

> Many of the letters we received were from relatives who only had themselves to provide the care, too fearful to leave their loved ones. ... Many had been full time carers now forced to watch as their loved one's body broke down. Dressings left unchanged and sores left to fester, nurses too busy to attend to even the basic of nursing needs. Many wrote how they watched their loved ones shrinking before them from lack of nourishment and care. (Cure the NHS, nd)

The incoming Conservative Government announced a public inquiry, to be chaired by Robert Francis, QC. Held during 2010 and 2011, it identified multiple examples of neglect and treatment (Francis, 2013). Patients were reported to have been left in urine-soaked sheets, treated roughly and given the wrong medication. Some were reported to have been so dehydrated that they had been reduced to drinking water from flower vases (BBC, 2019). The extent of the publicity was so high that it prompted a parliamentary response from Prime Minister David Cameron, rather than the health secretary as is normally the case. Drawing on the Francis report, Cameron argued that a culture had evolved in which 'patient care was always someone else's problem' and where managers ignored evidence of bad practice (Gov.uk, 2013).

While the Mid Staffordshire inquiry was in hearing, further abuse was revealed through the BBC's flagship documentary programme *Panorama* (BBC, 2011). The documentary came about after Terry Bryan, a nurse working at a Winterbourne View private hospital for people with learning disabilities, highlighted concerns to the BBC. Bryan had previously reported his concerns to the CQC but felt they had been ignored. The documentary adopted an undercover format, with the reporter getting a job as a healthcare worker at the hospital and secretly filming events. His footage showed patients with learning disabilities being slapped, taunted and dragged across the floor, and one person was shown being dragged into a shower fully clothed (Flynn, 2012). The prosecution of staff was reported widely in the newspapers, and the charity Mencap used the documentary to campaign for the closure of similar hospital assessment units.

The government responded to growing concerns about adult safeguarding through the Draft Care and Support Bill (HM Government, 2012). This led to the Care Act 2014, which was enacted in May of that year. Notably, in England, the government decided not to give practitioners new powers of entry. This decision was based on responses from the consultation on power of entry, which found that while the proposed measures were popular with professionals, they were unpopular with members of the public (Department of Health, 2013, para 32). Sections 42–47 of the Care Act 2014 provided a framework for how local authorities and other agencies should safeguard people at risk of abuse and neglect. Local authorities were given the lead responsibility for coordinating safeguarding, with each local authority instructed to establish a Safeguarding Adults Board in its area. The crux of local authority duties was contained within Section 42 of the Act, which required local authorities to consider whether there was reasonable cause to suspect if an adult had care and support needs, was experiencing, or at risk of, abuse and neglect and because of their needs was unable to protect themselves. In these cases, local authorities were given a duty to 'make (or cause to be made) whatever enquiries it thinks necessary to enable it to decide whether any action should be taken in the adult's case … and, if so, what and by whom' (Care Act 2014, Section 42(2)). The Act also instructed Safeguarding Adults Boards to conduct safeguarding adults reviews where specific failings in care were suspected, replacing the previous system of adult safeguarding case reviews. Part 2 of the Care Act 2014 focused on promoting new care standards in response to the Mid Staffordshire inquiry. The Act added to the 'duty of candour' in the Health and Social Care Act 2008 (Regulated Activities) Regulations 2014. This requires providers who are regulated under the CQC to be open and transparent with service users, their families and advocates where a 'notifiable safety incident' occurs.[4] The Act also increased the powers of the CQC, establishing three chief inspector roles focusing on hospitals, adult social care and general practice.

Several criticisms were made about the safeguarding powers within the Care Act 2014. Luke Clements, a professor of law, argued that the Act gave local authorities 'very little in terms of substance, to enhance their safeguarding powers' (2018, p 48). He noted that the Act did not define abuse, except through stating what financial abuse may involve (although definitions of abuse were included in the revised *Care and Support Statutory Guidance*) (DHSS, 2022). Gary Fitzgerald (2016), the chief executive of Action on Elder Abuse, observed that Section 42 of the Care Act 2014 was ambiguous, leading to differences in interpretation across local authorities. He argued that the descriptions of self-neglect given in the revised statutory guidance were unhelpful saying:

> It tells us that self-neglect may not prompt a section 42 enquiry and that this will depend 'on the adult's ability to protect themselves by controlling their own behaviour'. An adult deemed able to protect

themselves would not qualify for a safeguarding enquiry. But given that self-neglect is a behavioural condition, it is difficult to understand, let alone apply, such guidance. (Fitzgerald, 2016)

Research has also indicated that social workers continued to favour being given a statutory power of entry in adult safeguarding work, although they recognised that such powers might impact negatively on relationships with adults at risk and their families (Stevens et al, 2020).

From the beginning of the Care Act 2014 coming into force, concerns were expressed about the levels of safeguarding referrals. A 2016 *Community Care* article (McNicoll and Carter, 2016) reported on a LGA 'stocktake' which indicated that 103,900 referrals were made in the first 12 months of the Care Act 2014 coming into effect – this was reported as 'a substantial increase' on the previous year. Gary Fitzgerald said:

> If these figures are accurate, they represent a major increase in adult safeguarding intervention, and that must be welcomed because of what it means for victims. However, it is worth exploring the detail further as it is difficult to see how safeguarding teams effectively doubled their workloads at a time of substantial cutbacks. (Cited in McNicoll and Carter, 2016)

Despite criticisms from legal commentators, the new safeguarding powers were viewed in a positive light by those from the practice community. This may have been because the *Care and Support Statutory Guidance* (DHSC, 2022) gave a strong endorsement of the social work role (Whittington, 2016). Specifically, it viewed social workers as vital to safeguarding adults, recognising their ability to work with individuals in complex situations and to supervise safeguarding enquiries and lead safeguarding (paras 14.81). Additionally, the guidance endorsed the Making Safeguarding Personal approach, which had been driven by the LGA and ADASS, and it highlighted the role of principal social workers in applying it. In line with the guidance, the LGA and ADASS continued to promote the Making Safeguarding Personal initiative, conducting 'temperature checks' to assess its implementation and designing a new outcomes framework (Cooper et al, 2016).

Nonetheless, safeguarding duties under the Care Act 2014 pose a significant challenge for local authorities that are tasked with deciding whether the concerns they receive meet the criteria for a safeguarding enquiry. Government-collated statistics show that the number of safeguarding concerns received by local authorities (where a local authority is notified about a risk of abuse or neglect which could instigate a safeguarding enquiry) has risen steadily over the years. This number totalled 364,605 in the 12-month reporting period for 2016–17, and the figure reached 541,535 in

2021–22 (NHS Digital, 2022). Some research has suggested that the COVID-19 pandemic has been responsible for an increase in referrals in recent years (LGA, 2021). While this may be the case, the NHS Digital statistics indicate a rise in safeguarding referrals year on year since 2016–17. In 2020–21, 498,260 safeguarding concerns were received in England (equivalent to 1,121 per 100,000 adults). Of these, 152,270 resulted in a Section 42 enquiry, while 16,690 resulted in what NHS Digital calls an 'other enquiry' (where the adult did not meet all of the Section 41 Part 1 criteria, but where the local authority deemed it necessary to conduct a safeguarding enquiry; NHS Digital, 2020).

In summary, this period saw adult safeguarding placed on a statutory footing through the Care Act 2014. While the government had already begun consultations on a new adult safeguarding system in 2008, the Mid Staffordshire and Winterbourne View inquiries kept the abuse and neglect of adults in the public consciousness. The level of public attention to the issue made it difficult for the government to duck further reforms, with the Care Act 2014 providing powers designed to enable professionals to make enquiries into abuse in the community and enable new care standards in hospital. While groups like the ADASS had campaigned for greater statutory powers, these were withheld in England, though they were granted to practitioners in Scotland and Wales. Government statistics indicate a steep increase in safeguarding referrals. Reactions from the social work leaders and professionals suggest the Care Act 2014 was positively received by the profession, although whether that will remain the case is an open question.

Conclusion

This chapter, charting developments from the 1960s to the Care Act 2014 and after, has highlighted how the abuse and neglect of adults came to be seen as a social problem. According to Best (2013), claims-makers commonly seek media coverage to publicise their claims, which then filter down to the public and policy makers. This pattern can be seen in some parts of my social history but is less evident in others. Barbara Robb and AEGIS were successful in placing the problem of elder abuse on the political agenda. However, this attention was much more muted in the 1970s, with claims being limited to concerned medical practitioners in their professional journals. Adult abuse and neglect received some press attention throughout the 1980s, 1990s and 2000s, mainly though coverage of inquiries. Press attention then became more sustained from 2010, with the abuse and neglect of adults receiving regular press attention and a high degree of coverage. However, these cases did not act as a catalyst for the current safeguarding system. This work had already started through the *No Secrets* guidance (Department of Health, 2000) and the reviews of law and policy by the Law Commission and government committees which took place throughout the late 1990s and 2000s.

Best (2013) contends that claims-making leads to reactions from both the public and policy makers. While one would imagine that the public would disapprove of adult abuse and neglect, public surveys or research on this issue are rare, and it is difficult to know what public perceptions on the issue were or how they have evolved. Nonetheless, the evolution of national policies can be traced through an examination of policy documents. Claims-making in the 1960s led politicians to establish complaints procedures in the 1960s and 1970s. Those in the 1970s and 1980s led to *No Secrets* (Department of Health, 2000). Lobbying by professionals for new legal powers then led to the Care Act 2014.

According to Best's model, once policies have been made, agencies engage in social problem work. Policy makers set expectations which must be carried out, institutions frame expectations, and organisations employ workers to deal with the problem and monitor their work. This results in some individuals seeking attention from problem workers, and observers witnessing and commenting on these interactions. This may be commentated on by the media, who develop idealised versions of social problem work.

The final stage in the evolution of social problems, according to Best (2013), is policy outcomes. Several types of outcome are possible. Critics may argue that policies are ineffective or make the problems worse. Debates may occur as to how policy outcomes should be measured or judged. As I observed in the previous section, the duties and powers given to social workers under the Care Act 2014 were broadly welcomed by social work bodies. There has also been very little critical debate of these policies within the academic community. This stands in stark contrast to the situation in the child protection system, where criticism of legal frameworks by some practitioners and academics has been vociferous (Jones, 2018; Featherstone et al, 2019). There is also a shortage of literature focusing on how social workers view such work.

In the next chapter, I turn to the topic of social work and risk before exploring how social workers manage decisions about risk and safeguarding in my empirical chapters.

2

Risk and social work

Introduction

The previous chapter identified how understandings of adult safeguarding have evolved. The Care Act 2014 made safeguarding a statutory duty, with sections 42–47 focusing on 'safeguarding adults at risk of abuse and neglect'. Social workers are leading practitioners in this process as they are tasked with assessing and managing such risks. But what do we mean when we talk about risk? 'Risk' is a term which features heavily in social work practice. A search of social work textbooks and online resources reveals a wide range of materials on the subject, including advice on defining risk, using risk assessments and working with risk. Social workers in practice are likely to encounter risk every day, as the topic is a feature of assessments, care planning and court work. This is not to say that risk is seen as a universally good thing. Critical commentaries are common, with social workers and social work academics writing of the 'risks of risk management' (Barsky, 2015) and the dangers of 'feeding the risk monster' (Featherstone et al, 2018).

Current social work literature on risk broadly falls into three categories. First, there are books and articles which give practical advice about how social workers might, or ought, to 'do' risk, setting out various risk assessment and management tools. Second, there are books and articles which provide a critical commentary on risk, seeking to unpack the meanings that are attached to it. Third, there is the research literature, which explores how social workers negotiate the concept of risk 'on the ground' (Crath et al, 2023). There is, however, a shortage of research examining how social workers manage risk in practice within adult social work, with most studies focusing on child protection practice and to a lesser extent mental health.

While risk has become a central element of social work practice, we need to understand it within a broader framework. Risk is not just a dominant feature within social work; it is also a dominant feature within western societies. It has become an organising concept within science, economics and medicine. These disciplines all have their own knowledge about risk outlining how the risk is seen, measured or predicted.

As this book examines social work perceptions of risk within adult safeguarding work, this chapter sets the scene by outlining different ways of thinking about risk. In its narrowest sense, risk can be understood as the probability of an adverse event occurring during a stated period, or something which results from a particular challenge (Royal Society, 1992).

However, the meanings that we give to risk as a society are much broader than this and, in this chapter, I draw on the sociological literature that aims to unpack how the concept of risk is used in contemporary life. While sociology forms a part of most social work courses nowadays, it is unlikely that many social workers or social work students will be aware of this literature in much detail. I begin this chapter by setting out three of the most influential risk theories: Ulrich Beck's theories on 'risk society'; governmentality theory, which draws and expands on the work of Michel Foucault; and Mary Douglas' work on risk and culture. I outline these theories here because social work academics often refer to them when making arguments about changes to the welfare state and social work practice. I then move on to explore an emerging area in the sociology of risk and uncertainty – that of 'risk work', which focuses on how individuals interpret and work with rules and regulations about risk. Having done this, I set out how social work academics have explained the rise of risk thinking within social care settings, drawing on risk theories. Finally, I use the framework of risk work to identify what research evidence tells us about how social workers assess and manage risk in adult care.

Key risk theories

Risk society

A frequent contention made within the social work risk literature is that 'risk has replaced need' within the social services sector (Webb, 2006; Green, 2007; Alfandari et al, 2023). This statement is heavily influenced by the work of Ulrich Beck, who offers a broad overarching theory that aims to explain changes in 'modernity'. In sociology, the term 'modernity' is used to refer to the period of change from traditional, rural or agrarian societies to secular, urban or industrial ones (Cohen, 2006). Beck argues that we are transitioning to a period of 'second modernity', which he terms 'risk society' (see Beck, 1992; Beck and Grande, 2010). From this perspective, 'first modernity' was a period in which the social order was relatively stable. Wealth in this period was driven by industrial production. Identities were based around notions of class. People had faith that science was linked to progress, and nation states were in control of their own terrains. However, Beck argues that the risks and dangers created by modernity have spiralled out of control. Such changes have led to a second form of modernity, which he terms 'risk society'.

A central theme within Beck's (1992) writing is that we are facing a new form of risk, which has arisen from the first stage of modernity. While dangers have always existed within society, these were largely caused by nature – for example, floods or famine. Beck sees risks as being distinct from dangers in that the former are 'manufactured' or 'fabricated' (1996b, p 5). In other words, risks were created by humans with a view to making technological progress. For example, during the first period of modernity, governments aimed to solve problems such as poverty or famine through scientific or technological solutions. However, while new technologies (such as chemical engineering and nuclear power) were intended to increase production, these led to new forms of risk which society has become focused around. These new risks are different in form and character from the previous dangers as they are 'intangible', meaning that they may not be immediately sensed (Beck, 1996b, p 5). For example, radiation is harmful to humans, animals and nature, but cannot be tasted, seen or smelled. Consequently, society is forced to rely on science to detect them, but this too has problems. Risks may not be immediately visible, even to those with scientific expertise, and the scale of risks have grown. Certain risks arising from processes such as nuclear power or global warming may have catastrophic and irreversible effects on nature and the environment. These risks cross national boundaries, making it difficult for states to control them. It may also be difficult to pinpoint who has generated them (Beck et al, 2003). While factors such as personal wealth may offer some protection to individuals, it is not possible to escape these risks completely, as environmental risks (such as smog) affect everyone – as Beck puts it, 'poverty is hierarchic, smog is democratic' (1992, p 36). Beck contends that an awareness of these risks has led to a cultural change in which societies become less concerned with the production of 'goods' and more concerned with the production of 'bads', leading to an increased focus on how to control the latter (Beck, 1992, p 49). This leads society to engage in a process of self-confrontation referred to as 'reflexive modernisation'; here, concerns about the creation or use of technologies are eclipsed by worries about how actual or potential risks may be managed (Beck, 1996a, p 28). It also leads to new alliances between groups or individuals now sceptical of the old social order, and the creation of new roles or agencies with a focus on risk management.

While concerns about threats to the ecology are central to Beck's work, his writing seeks to explain public attitudes to risk, which have relevance to professionals. He argues that as risk becomes a central concern of contemporary society, the public demands that experts and policy makers take steps to control it. However, this process is rarely straightforward. Experts may be divided about how risks should be managed, and ongoing failures to predict risks may lead to experts and governments appearing impotent. This problem was outlined in an earlier text by Giddens, who noted that '[w]idespread knowledge of risk environments leads to awareness of the limits of expertise and forms one of the "public relations" problems that has to be faced by those who seek to sustain lay trust in expert systems' (1990, p 130). This leads to a paradox in which the public increasingly lacks trust in these parties while at the same time demanding that they take more measures to limit risk.

Beck also sees risk society as bringing about significant changes in relation to group identity. He argues that the transition to a 'risk society' sees the logics of the previous form of modernity being interrogated or questioned (Beck, 1992). This then leads to a process of 'individualisation', in which ideas about social class and the division of labour are re-examined, with individuals increasingly defining themselves according to alternative categories, such as ethnicity, gender, age or nationality (Beck, 1992; Beck and Beck-Gernsheim, 2002). While the possibility of new identities is potentially liberating, individuals are also faced with loss of stability as traditional categories become weaker. Consequently, individuals 'must produce, stage and cobble together their biographies themselves' (Beck, 1997, p 95) and, in doing so, must learn to navigate the changing demands of social institutions, such as state institutions, education systems, work, social networks and family. Such processes place many of the burdens of risk management on individuals, with the role of the state being reduced.

Governmentality

The second theory applied to the study of risk that I consider here is that of governmentality. This set of ideas was first set out by Foucault (1991) and has been developed and applied to the concept of risk by several other authors (Rose et al, 2006; Dean, 2010; Roberts, 2019). Foucault described this theory in lectures to the Collège de France (Foucault, 1991) in which he spoke about the changes which had taken place in the way that European sovereigns or rulers governed populations between the 16th and 18th centuries. Foucault notes that the Enlightenment and the Reformation led to shifts in thinking about how power should be exercised, with a new literature focusing on the 'art of government' (Foucault, 1991, p 89). These writings argue that good governance involves 'the right disposition of things' or, put more simply, a system which promotes the welfare of the population (Foucault, 1991, p 93). Old forms of governance, in which sovereigns aimed to enforce compliance through public displays of punishment, were gradually replaced. These shifts occurred because, as writings on the art of government identify, aspects of society, such as the 'population' or 'economy', have their own laws and patterns and new expert knowledge was needed to manage them (Foucault, 1991, p 99). This then led to sovereigns devolving some powers to professionals and other groups, such as medics or economists. Professional knowledge came to be used to define how the population should be governed towards the greater good, with individuals being encouraged to draw on such knowledge to manage their own behaviour. We can understand how this works in practice by thinking about how health campaigns are used to influence our behaviours. Public health campaigns aim to improve the health of the population by drawing on medical and nutritional research and passing this knowledge down to individuals in a digestible form. Government adverts and information leaflets encouraging us to eat more fruit and vegetables and to exercise regularly are, in effect, asking us to pay more attention to the way we look after ourselves. Governmentality theorists see the use of such professional knowledge as significant because it aims to affect subjectivity – that is, the way people see the world. As Rose (1989) argues, government strategies target the 'soul' of the individual, with governance being achieved through sovereign powers (powers of command) as well as disciplinary powers (which seek to shape subjectivity and habits).

While governmentality is not primarily a theory about risk, several authors identify risk assessment and management as a central 'technology of government' (Castel, 1991; Defert, 1991; Ewald, 1991; Roberts, 2019; Weber and McCulloch, 2019; Bevan, 2021; Wilkins and Gobby, 2022). These writers argue that risk is not something which is intrinsically 'real', but rather something that demonstrates how problems are 'imagined' and then managed within societies. Drawing on the example of insurance, governmentality theorists argue that risk is viewed through the prism of statistics and probability (see Booth, 2021). With car insurance, large amounts of data (statistics) are collected by insurance companies and used to calculate which groups are most likely to make a claim (probability). Furthermore, the insurance system establishes that different types of accident should result in different levels of compensation, allowing risks to be pooled among all those who take out insurance premiums. Insurance companies may establish that young people are more likely to be involved in a car accident than older people, or that people in inner cities are more likely to have their car broken into than people in the suburbs. Such information is used to calculate how much drivers should be charged and whether their insurance premiums should go up or down. Such procedures are not static and may be used and adapted in different ways according to the situation (Ewald, 1991; Booth, 2021).

Governmentality theorists have focused on the ways new technologies or procedures affect how professionals and members of the public are expected to manage risk. Drawing on Foucault's theories, Castel (1991) sets out how risk technologies might affect professional risk practices within the field of welfare – specifically, psychiatry. Castel argues that in the 1960s, psychiatry in the United States started to develop a new model of practice, based on statistics. This marked a shift from a system in which psychiatrists aimed to manage 'dangerous' behaviours at the individual level to one in which they considered levels of psychiatric risk across the population (Castel, 1991, p 283). For example, under the former system, when a concern was raised about a dangerous person, a psychiatrist would conduct an individual assessment on them. The assessment would seek to establish whether the person was likely to pose a danger to themselves or others. Where this was the case, the psychiatrist might recommend hospital treatment to manage the danger. New patterns of risk thinking differed from this, in that professionals became concerned with assessing the likelihood of negative events (risks) occurring within the population. In practice, this meant that rather than assessing dangerousness at the individual level, psychiatrists began to use statistical data to calculate which groups of people were likely to become unwell or display 'undesirable modes of behaviour in the future' (Castel, 1991, p 287). This then allowed professionals to use measures aiming to influence and change behaviours at the population level, lessening the need for face-to-face contact with service users. Castel provides an illustration of this:

> The presence of some, or a certain number, of these factors of risk sets off an automatic alert. That is to say, a specialist social worker for example, will be sent to the family to confirm or disconfirm the real presence of a danger, on the basis of a probabilistic and abstract existence of risks. One does not *start from* a conflictual situation observable in experience, rather one deduces it from a general definition one wishes to prevent. (1991, pp 287–8)

Castel's theories are useful in showing how statistics drawn from the population might alter practice. However, it has been noted that Castel somewhat overstated his case (Godin, 2004) and that while statistics may influence who services are targeted at, face-to-face practice remains necessary – though its frequency may be reduced.

In addition to focusing on professional risk practices, governmentality theorists have also highlighted how individuals increasingly come to be held responsible for managing their own risks. This 'responsibilisation' refers to situations where people have been given responsibility for 'a task which previously would have been the responsibility of another – usually a state agency' (O'Malley, 2009, p 277). These processes are closely aligned to concepts of autonomy and choice within 'neoliberal' societies (Juhila and Raitakari, 2016). While the concept of neoliberalism is contested, it is generally used to refer to policies emphasising the responsibilities of individuals over those of the state and is aligned to reductions in state spending, an increased role for the private sector and a faith in 'market forces'. Within neoliberal frameworks, choice is portrayed in policy statements as a virtue and used to suggest that power has been transferred from the state to the individual. However, people are asked to make decisions about their welfare against 'a web of vocabularies, injunctions, promises, dire warnings and threats of intervention, organized increasingly around a proliferation of norms' (Miller and Rose, 2008, p 205). Where individuals are seen to have failed to manage risks effectively, health and welfare professionals may step in with a view to acting on the person's behalf or re-educating them about how they should exercise their responsibilities effectively.

Cultural theory of risk

A third influential theory which attempts to account for risk is Mary Douglas' cultural theory. A central theme within Douglas' work is that people's views about risk are heavily influenced by culture. Douglas is critical of psychological theories of risk, which focus on how people make choices based on their individual perceptions. While she believes that lay people consider factors like probability when making risk judgements, she argues that people 'come already primed with culturally learned assumptions and weightings' (Douglas, 1992, p 58). For this reason, she feels that culture needs to be examined to understand risk thinking.

Douglas' work on risk is influenced by her earlier work, most notably *Purity and Danger* (1966), in which she focuses on the concepts of purity and pollution or taboo, which she sees as a key theme within societies. Douglas takes a comparative approach by contrasting how concepts of purity and pollution were viewed across what she terms 'primitive' and 'advanced' societies (Douglas, 1966). While her language is now outmoded, her intent is to demonstrate that these concepts are informed by cultural ideas or norms rather than by scientific fact. A key theme for Douglas is that 'dirt is matter out of place' (1966, p 44). For example, grass may be viewed as clean in the garden but as dirt when on the dining room table. Similarly, sauce may be viewed as clean in the bottle but as dirt if it is splashed on a pair of trousers (see Lupton, 1999). Rituals of identifying taboo or impure substances and purifying them therefore act to contain disorder within societies and build a sense of social unity. Douglas argues that the contemporary concern with things being clean or unclean has replaced the traditional concern with the 'sacred and profane' (1966, p 161), with the role of classification being central. As Arnoldi argues, 'risk, in Douglas's view, is the threat of the classificationary system being thrown out of kilter', with such a breach viewed as a moral transgression (2009, p 39). Building on arguments from *Purity and Danger* (1966), Douglas sees the concept of risk as replacing traditional concepts of taboo or sin, as a result of society becoming more individualistic and therefore less responsive to traditional moral notions (Douglas, 1992, p 26). Consequently, notions of risk focus heavily on violation of the rights of the individual. They are concerned with identifying the cause or person responsible for the risk and, in some cases, meting out punishment (Linsley and Shrives, 2009). A central focus of cultural theory is therefore on perceptions of risks, including judgements about which risks are most severe and who should be held responsible for them (Douglas, 1992). In one of her most-quoted passages, Douglas argues that 'in all places at all times the universe is moralized and politicized. Disasters that befoul the air and soil and poison the water are generally turned to political account: someone already unpopular is going to get the blame' (1992, p 5).

A central point within cultural theory is that perceptions of risk, including which risks are viewed as being the gravest and who should be held responsible for them, are strongly influenced by both classificationary systems and cultural norms within a given culture (Douglas and Wildavsky, 1982). Douglas states that different types of people may have different capacities to respond to risk, depending on their place within (or outside) organisational dynamics. Douglas and her collaborators made efforts to explain how organisational and institutional responses affected how risk is categorised.

The 'grid' element of Douglas' model represents the amount of autonomy or freedom that an individual may have to choose their roles in society. Individuals on the low end of the grid are seen as autonomous, having significant freedoms to choose their social roles. By contrast, those who are on the high end face high levels of restriction on their ability to choose their social roles. These restrictions may be caused by a range of factors, such as gender, ethnicity or class (Rayner, 1992). The 'group' element of the model refers to the degree of social cohesion between individuals. Those with low group ties have weak social bonds and largely act separately from one another, although they may come together for specific purposes. Those with high group ties live in cultures with high levels of social cohesion, where people are more likely to act as a community rather than as individuals.

The grid/group model outlines the characteristics of four different group cultures: individualist, egalitarian, hierarchist and fatalist. Individualist cultures are 'low group' and 'low grid'. In these cultures, individuals may work together when collaboration could lead to individual gain (Linsley and Shrives, 2009). They have high levels of competition and espouse principles of self-regulation within a free-market ethos. Within such cultures, risk is viewed as an opportunity for individuals to make gains through entrepreneurship. Consequently, self-regulation is espoused over regulation by the state or other organisations (Linsley and Shrives, 2009).

Egalitarian cultures are 'high group' and 'high grid'. In these groups, the wellbeing of the group is given priority over the wellbeing of the individual, with the society highlighting ideals such as equality and justice (Linsley and Shrives, 2009). Within such groups, value is placed on the need for individuals to help each other on a voluntary basis, and a sharp distinction is made between members of the group and outsiders (Douglas, 1982). Risk is seen as emanating from outsiders, and suspicion is voiced about the expert status of professionals (Linsley and Shrives, 2009).

Hierarchist cultures are 'high grid' and 'high group'. In such societies, there are highly defined group boundaries and limitations on the social roles group members may opt for (McCreadie et al, 2008). Here, authority is respected and value is placed on traditions and customs, with outsiders mistrusted because they may challenge established boundaries. Professional status is also respected, and professionals are looked to for judgements about risk.

Fatalist cultures are 'high grid' and 'low group'. In these societies, individuals are highly constrained when it comes to the roles they may adopt and have little self-determination (Linsley and Shrives, 2009). There is limited bonding between people, meaning that individuals are left to their own fate. Consequently, there is little formal management of risk, with individuals experiencing dangers or setbacks according to fate.

Readers might wonder why it is necessary to categorise group cultures in this way. Douglas' model is useful because it aims to make explicit the cultural biases that inform assumptions about which actions are appropriate and which are not (Stoltz, 2014). These assumptions are often implicit and may be presented as 'common sense'. Consequently, when seeking to understand how policy makers or professional groups respond to risk, it is helpful to consider how cultural assumptions might drive their views.

Risk work

The three theories discussed in the previous section provide different ways of thinking about why risk has become such a dominant theme within contemporary society. Each theory provides a different take on risk. Beck's theory suggests that our preoccupation with risk reflects changes in society and the way it has come to be organised. Governmentality theory sees risk as a form of governance and as one means through which problems come to be 'imagined' and solutions enforced. Douglas' theory identifies how the concept of risk is used to highlight things which are unacceptable or taboo. While each theory provides a broad overview of how risk is understood and dealt with, the founders of these theories did not deal with how people work with risk on a day-to-day basis. Several research studies have looked at how patients understand risk or how organisations manage it; however, research focusing on the views and practices of health and social care professionals is much less common (Gale et al, 2016). For this reason, there has been a growing interest in how professionals manage risk and uncertainty – an area now known as 'risk work'.

The term 'risk work', first used by Tom Horlick-Jones (2005), is used to describe research which focuses on how professionals manage working practices that relate to risk in some way. According to Horlick-Jones, a new field of study focusing on risk work is necessary because existing theories do not do justice to this issue. He thinks that broad-ranging, but abstract, theories of risk (such as Beck's risk society or governmentality) do not help us to understand the 'diversity of risk-related practices that may be observed in real-world settings' (Horlick-Jones, 2005, p 296). Despite taking this line, he acknowledges that some of the points made by these theorists are useful. For example, he agrees with Beck's view that risk has become an important feature of everyday life and that public and private organisations have become 'saturated by the language of risk and the application of risk techniques' (Horlick-Jones, 2005, p 294). He also thinks that risk tools could be used as a form of surveillance (as claimed by governmentality theorists) and might be used to monitor and control professional decision-making. However, Horlick-Jones feels that there is a need to study how risk is understood by different people (such as professionals and lay people) in different settings. Drawing on Douglas (1992), he notes that risk decisions are inherently political, as they rely on normative values about which actions are right or wrong. These values are not always obvious, as the measurement and management of risk is often presented as being scientific or objective. For example, the Royal Society defines risk as 'the probability that a particular adverse event occurs during a stated period of time, or results in a particular challenge' (1992, p 2). However, even where such measures are used, negative and positive values denote situations that are problematic and require intervention (and therefore have moral implications; Heyman et al, 2012). Consequently, Horlick-Jones thinks that it is important to understand both institutional risk practices and the way individuals interpret them. These dynamics become important when understanding how professionals exercise power in professions like police work. Drawing on Bittner (1967), Horlick-Jones (2005b) argues that policing is not conducted solely in line with law and policy, but draws also on officers' discretion. Information gathering might take place alongside informal enforcement activities, such as threats. Officers may also engage in trade-offs in which one risk might be allowed to prevent a larger risk from occurring. For example, Horlick-Jones (2001, 2005b) observed that when policing the Notting Hill Carnival, officers chose to deal with some infractions of the law later.

Risk assessment and management tools have been heavily promoted within health and social care. Risk tools promote ways of thinking about problems which appear to offer professionals a means to make judgements that are efficient, authoritative and objective (Rose, 1999). In doing so, they draw on societal expectations that 'rational' strategies for managing risk (drawing on scientific or technical knowledge) are preferred (Zinn, 2008). However, there are gaps between such expectations and what can be delivered in practice. Risk assessments calculate probabilities by drawing on large amounts of research data. Because some events are rare, there may not be enough data to make accurate predictions. Also practitioners may have to make quick decisions and so may not have time to evaluate the research data. Consequently, workers may draw on 'non-rational strategies', such as belief, hope and faith, or 'in between strategies', such as trust, intuition or emotion (Zinn, 2008). Given the limitations practitioners face in their day-to-day work, rational, non-rational and in between strategies should all be viewed as reasonable ways of managing risk (Zinn, 2016). The challenge for researchers is to work out which strategies practitioners use in which circumstances.

So, what do we currently know about how health and social care professionals make decisions about risk in practice? A review of research literature (Gale et al, 2016) has found three central components to risk work. First, professionals are involved in 'translating risks'. Many risk assessments draw on abstract statistical data to calculate the probability of something occurring. To make such data meaningful, professionals need to apply it to the cases they are working with. They also need to be able to explain their reasoning to service users to build and maintain trust. As statistical data is not always available, workers may also draw on other strategies, such as personal experience or intuition, to manage uncertainty. Second, research indicates that 'minimising risk' is a central component of risk work. This involves encouraging or supporting changes of behaviour in the service user, providing interventions or creating new policies and procedures. The question of who is responsible for managing risk is central to such work. Some risks may be viewed as the responsibility of the state (such as managing communicable diseases), whereas other risks may be seen as the responsibility of service users (such as collecting and taking prescribed medication). In the latter case, risk work may involve educating the person about the risk or holding them responsible for problem behaviours. Third, 'caring in the context of risk' is an important part of risk work. This type of work focuses on service users facing uncertainty about their health or social circumstances. Care may involve supporting service users to make choices or providing them with emotional support once they have received risk information.

Drawing on the literature review mentioned earlier (Gale et al, 2016), Brown and Gale (2018b) conclude that there are three components to risk work, which they present in the form of a triangle. Risk work is dependent on workers using 'risk knowledge', which forms the first part of the triangle. For risk assessments that draw on large amounts of research data, workers are required to interpret the results and may use alternative knowledge to complement or challenge the actions they suggest in specific situations. Abstract risk knowledge is therefore re-embedded in processes of 'interventions' to manage or reduce the risk. This is the second point of the triangle. Such interventions may involve a professional informing or advising a service user about risk as well as undertaking or reviewing risk assessments. Risk knowledge and risk interventions are, in turn, informed by and reliant on 'social relations' (that is, relationships between two or more individuals) and so need to be understood with these social dynamics in mind. This is the third point in the triangle. Workers may experience difficulties when applying risk knowledge or risk interventions to individual cases due to 'ecological and inductive prevention paradoxes' (difficulties applying the data to real-world situations; Brown and Gale, 2018b, p 5). For example, mental health professionals may struggle to know how an offender with mental health problems may manage in the community in cases where they have been detained in hospital for several years (Heyman et al, 2013). These issues lead to moral- and role-related dilemmas. The question of how much freedom to give an older adult to transfer independently is not just a technical issue; it also raises questions about the person's autonomy, which in turn impact on judgements about what should be done and which professionals should be involved. Also, tensions exist between risk knowledge and social relations. Health and social care professionals are required to assess risk, but must balance this against other elements of their role, such as providing support to users in an empathic manner. These issues may lead to tensions around trust and openness between parties, with the short-term implications of intervention needing to be balanced with the longer-term impact on trust and the professional–client relationship.

Drawing on the risk work literature, there is a strong case for studying how professionals manage risk in everyday practice. To consider this, I set out how risk has been theorised within the social work literature, then consider how social work and risk work theories can be applied to the study of adult safeguarding.

Social work and risk

As this book focuses on the management of risk and uncertainty within social work, it is important to consider how risk theories have been applied by social work writers. While it would be useful to explain how these writers have applied the theories of Beck, Foucault, Douglas' and other scholars one by one, this is not easily achieved. Social work academics have tended to fuse these ideas together, so it is difficult to draw clear lines between theories. However, several themes re-emerge frequently within the social work risk literature, and I set these out here.

Social work theorists have generally agreed with Beck's (1992) contention that we are living in a risk society. Social work is seen to mirror the attitudes of wider society, which is increasingly concerned with valuing safety. Because of this, there are growing expectations that social workers will act to monitor and manage risk. The degree to which workers have done this has been a frequent point of debate in the media. As Butler and Drakeford (2011) note, social work has been 'on trial' since the 1970s, with various inquiries focusing on the adequacy of professional practice. These inquiries have found the profession wanting, leading to ever more regulatory frameworks and bureaucratic procedures designed to ensure practitioners assess and manage risk. For these reasons, several writers argue that the topic of risk has come to dominate social work practice (Kemshall, 2001, 2010; Webb, 2006; Green,

2007; Alfandari et al, 2023). These shifts are viewed as significant because they threaten 'the humane project of social work', concerned with the moral values of care, trust, kindness and respect (Broadhurst et al, 2010, p 1047). They are also seen as limiting the exercise of professional judgement and as stifling innovation within social work organisations (Munro, 2004; Brown, 2010).

While there is general agreement that contemporary social work practice reflects the concerns of 'risk society', several authors have attempted to trace how we got here through drawing on the work of risk theorists and applying this to social work. A dominant theme within the risk literature is that risk narratives arose due to shifts in welfare policy from the 1970s onwards. During this period, there was a challenge to what has been termed the post-war 'consensus' (Dutton, 1997), which is seen to have existed between 1945 and the late 1970s. The origins of the post-war consensus in the UK are seen to lie in the Beveridge report (1942), which led to the founding of the welfare state. During this time, there was broad agreement across political parties in favour of universal welfare provision, namely the NHS, expanded education and government housing programmes. The 1970s saw a break from this consensus with a shift towards a 'residualist' social policy (Kemshall, 2016). Under this logic, the provision of welfare was viewed as a last resort when support could not be provided by families or the voluntary sector. In the UK, these policies were first associated with Thatcher's government and are often identified as neoliberal. From a neoliberal perspective, universal welfare policies are problematic because they are abused by 'feckless individuals' (Barry, 1990) and create perverse incentives, encouraging welfare dependence (see Giddens, 1998). The shrinking of the welfare state is viewed as a corrective to this trend, with a residual or minimal safety net model replacing a universal one. These shifts have been aligned with the process of responsibilisation, in that people are compelled to monitor and manage risks in their own lives, with social workers being made responsible for risk management where they are unable or unwilling to do so (Ferguson, 2007; Raitakari et al, 2019). This then shifts the moral foundations on which social work operates. As Webb notes:

> for neo-liberalism the principle of the 'common good' which provided a justification for early social work can no longer be tied with 'the social'. The advanced liberal programme of governance constructs politics not through normative appeals to the greater good of society, but through the rational ordering of the calculating, private choices of entrepreneurial individuals. (2006, p 54)

Due to changes in the welfare state, the concept of risk has been linked to notions of choice. Specifically, it is argued that framings of choice within contemporary welfare regimes have led to a rise in risk thinking. At first sight, this might seem an odd claim, as notions of choice and control are often associated with empowerment within social work. However, neoliberal framings of choice have been viewed as problematic because they are seen to have undermined universal welfare regimes. Universal welfare can be viewed as a contract between the state and individuals, where the assumption is that individuals will lead a prudent life in exchange for state protections against uncertainty (Rose, 1996). Neoliberal regimes, by contrast, employ the logics of the market to encourage individuals to take responsibility for themselves. Because individuals are compelled to choose from a range of services (such as schools, hospitals or nursing homes) in order to obtain what would once have been social benefits (such as educational advantage, good health status and contentment in old age), neoliberalism is associated with the process of responsibilisation (Rose, 1996). In other words, individuals are seen as being at least partially to blame in instances where they fail to make the right choices, and professionals are tasked with taking control where individuals are unable or unwilling to do so. For this reason, processes such as care planning and personalisation (focusing on early intervention and service user control over the services they receive) are viewed critically by some (Kemshall, 2010; Scourfield, 2010; Carey, 2022).

New forms of individual responsibility are viewed as a risk issue because the burden of managing health and welfare risks is placed with individuals and consequently linked to concerns about responsibilisation (Ferguson, 2007; Raitakari et al, 2019). While some social work academics have been critical of this trend, it is worth noting that others have focused on the way in which risk taking may empower individuals (see Zinn, 2020). For example, Duffy (2010) argues that personal budgets, self-directed support and personal planning should be viewed as 'technologies of care' which can be used to promote social justice. Similarly, Carr (2012) maintains that personalisation policies are congruent with social work values as they promote self-determination among adults.

In addition to this, several authors have argued that western governments have decentralised welfare responsibilities, passing increasing responsibility on to a range of agencies, such as local authorities, voluntary agencies and the private sector organisations (Rothstein, 2006). These societal changes led to the creation of 'new public management' procedures designed to improve efficiency and performance and to protect consumers (Green and Sawyer, 2010). These processes are promoted by governments on the basis that they create greater transparency, but they create tensions for providers who are tasked with delivering the service (Rothstein, 2006). These tensions then tend to be framed as risks. Such interpretations of risks are wide ranging and may apply to risks to service users, risks to governance procedures and reputational risks to agencies or professionals (Green and Sawyer, 2010).

Within health and social care settings, such risks are increasingly managed through risk assessment processes. For this reason, much of the social work literature has focused on the strengths and weaknesses of different risk assessment processes. Three main types of risk assessment tools have been identified in the literature; 'clinical assessments', 'actuarial assessments' and 'informed professional judgement' (Dixon and Robb, 2016). Clinical assessments involve a practitioner making a professional judgement about the likelihood of a person posing a danger to themselves or to others. Such judgements are made on a case-by-case basis and rely on the skills of the practitioner to identify risks and solutions. These assessments give professionals a high degree of freedom but have been criticised for being subjective, leading to high levels of inaccuracy (Milner and Campbell, 1995). Actuarial risk assessments adopt a different approach through using a, 'formal, algorithmic, objective procedure (for example, an equation) to reach a decision' (Grove and Meehl, 1996, p 293). The term 'actuarial' comes from the insurance industry, where an actuary is a person who calculates the probability of future events, which then informs how much people are charged for their insurance. Actuarial assessments draw on a range of risk factors (such as age, gender, offending history or mental health diagnosis) to calculate the likelihood of an event occurring in the future (such as violence towards others). While these tools claim to predict risk, they can be better be understood as probability statements (Canton et al, 2005). As such, they have certain limits. Many of the measurements used are static (such as gender or age), meaning that assessments can overlook individual factors. In addition, because actuarial assessments generate predictions, there is a chance that they may generate what is known as 'false positives' (where an assessment indicates a risk that does not exist) or 'false negatives' (where an assessment fails to identify a present risk). Informed professional judgements on the other hand, combine actuarial assessments and clinical approaches. They do this through generating probability statements while also allowing practitioners greater freedom to make judgements, based on individual or contextual factors.

Much has been written about the threat that actuarial thinking poses to social work (Webb, 2006; Green, 2007; Pollack, 2010). Webb (2009) argues that actuarial thinking has 'recast' the nature of social work. In his view, actuarial practices have come to underpin the way that welfare problems are thought about and managed in western societies, such as the UK. These practices are based on several government suppositions: first, that it is possible to predict the future behaviour of an individual by drawing on data which records the past behaviour of a population; second, that judgements drawing on objective evidence, such as statistics, are more accurate than subjective evidence, such as the views of individuals; and, third, outcomes within the welfare sector will be improved if statistical information is given priority over other sources of information. In Webb's view (2006, 2009), these suppositions are damaging to social work practice because they deny the importance of social factors when it comes to welfare problems. They are also seen to underplay the importance of relationships within social work practice by implying that greater focus should be given to measuring and monitoring future behaviours. While such arguments about actuarialism have been influential in the social work literature, they tend to oversimplify the range of risk practices that have been developed. It has long been noted that actuarial risk assessments have limitations (Doyle and Dolan, 2002), and researchers arguing for actuarial assessments to be used in a pure way tend to be the exception, not the rule. Furthermore, the argument that government risk practices are underpinned by the logics of actuarialism overlooks the fact that governments have acknowledged the limitations for some time and tend to promote holistic models. For example, *Best Practice in Managing Risk* (Department of Health, 2009), a document setting out risk assessment practices in the mental health sector, argues that actuarial tools should inform professional judgement rather than replacing it. In some areas of practice, such as learning disabilities services, there is little evidence of actuarial tools being used, with most assessments drawing on professional judgement (Dixon and Robb, 2016).

Although much has been written about risk reduction, there is also a growing literature focusing on the benefits of 'positive risk taking'. This comes from a concern among professionals that they are being expected to simply 'wrap people up in cotton wool' – to keep them safe and sound, away from any possible harm' (care worker, cited in Titterton, 2004, p 11). Several research projects solidified this claim, noting that early policy encouraged practitioners to focus on safe outcomes rather than getting involved with decisions about risk (Seale et al, 2013; Hollomotz, 2014). Subsequent policy recognised this problem and placed emphasis on the need for service users to be encouraged to take positive risks (Department of Health, 2009). Practice models within social services and health have focused on ways of promoting positive risk taking through greater involvement of service users within the risk assessment process (Titterton, 2011; Taylor and McKeown, 2013; Felton et al, 2017) and by focusing on creative solutions (Seale et al, 2013).

In addition to charting the logics of risk assessment, social work academics have also focused on the way that risk has been linked to accountability and blame in their practice. Drawing on Douglas (1992), these writers note that risk may be used as a resource within society to identify taboo behaviours and to allocate responsibility for them. Parton (1996) draws attention to expectations by policy makers that social work should be concerned with identifying high-risk cases or high-risk situations, and that interventions should be targeted accordingly. These expectations are enforced through processes of regulation, namely audits and inquiries. Both mechanisms have the effect of shaping future practice. Audits have the function of making experts accountable for their actions, thereby narrowing professional discretion. Inquiries seek to establish 'what went wrong', but can also be viewed as a means of reassuring the public through providing an official response to scandal in which certain groups are blamed while others are protected (Warner, 2006). While inquiries may prompt feelings of shame in those individuals who are held to account (Hardy, 2020), they also shape social work practice by raising anxiety in workers (Warner, 2006). This encourages workers to focus on risk reduction, but may also encourage defensive practice. Press reports may have a similar effect through labelling social workers either 'overzealous do-gooding meddlers' or 'gullible wimps' (Warner, 2013).

In summary, several points can be made about the theoretical social work literature as it stands. Risk is seen to have become a core component of social work practice. This focus is often seen to have been driven by neoliberal policy agendas. These agendas place the responsibility for measuring and managing risk with the service users, thereby undermining universal welfare policies. Several theorists also argue that assessment tools limit worker discretion, with risk reduction or elimination being the name of the game. While such perspectives have gained a lot of traction within the social work literature, several problems should be noted. Critical theorists tend to frame all risk practices as a regrettable part of contemporary life. For example, in his book *Social Work in a Risk Society*, Webb (2006) sees risk practices as upholding neoliberal values and concludes that they should be wholly resisted by the profession. A problem with such arguments is that they fail to acknowledge that risk tools can have any utility. As Hardy argues, 'the suggestion that the rise of risk has had a detrimental effect on practice rests on the assumption of a dichotomous opposition between care and control' (2015, p 197). Some social workers may believe that social work should be purely about providing support, and they have no role in assessing or preventing risk, although they are likely to be in the minority. Furthermore, there has been an increased emphasis on positive risk taking (Titterton, 2011; Seale et al, 2013), although workers need to make such decisions in the context of a system which is apt to blame them for any errors. As safeguarding remains a core part of social work practice, it is important for us to understand how social workers make decisions about risk in practice. In this light, the following section considers how we might examine such practice theoretically through using the concept of risk work.

Adult social work and risk work

As we saw in the previous section, some theorists argue that the concept of choice has been used by policy makers to transfer the responsibility for risk management to individuals. These authors argue that individuals are encouraged to manage their own risks, with professionals such as social workers being called on where the person is unable or unwilling to do so. These theoretical arguments have been influential, but we need to consider whether they are supported by research evidence. To examine this, the section looks at the current evidence to examine what we know about how social workers make adult safeguarding decisions in practice. To organise the section, I use Brown and Gale's (2018b) model of risk work, highlighting how social workers apply risk knowledge, how they use interventions and how social relations affect this work.

First, let us consider how social workers use risk knowledge in adult safeguarding work. Research in this area is limited. However, current studies examining how social care and health professionals understand risk have found that judgements about risk are linked to legal and policy concepts such as 'proportionality', 'best interests' and 'liberty', which frame the way risk is interpreted (Stevenson and Taylor, 2017). For example, when discussing the risks related to direct payments in adult care, social workers and their managers stressed the importance of balancing risk and choice (Stevens et al, 2018). This balance was not viewed as straightforward as the policy objectives of safeguarding and personalisation were seen to be at odds with one another. Workers used probabilistic phrases, such as 'potential', 'probable' or 'highly likely', to talk about risk in meetings or reports (Stevenson and Taylor, 2017). However, these terms were used subjectively rather than scientifically, with risk management cultures within teams shaping the ways in which risk was defined.

Second, let us consider how interventions affect adult safeguarding work. Interventions can be understood as frameworks or practices which may emerge because of new risk knowledge or due to new policy concerns (Brown and Gale, 2018b). Current research suggests that adult safeguarding practice has been primarily driven by policy concerns at both local and national levels, rather than by new risk knowledge. In the following section I use risk interventions to refer to adult safeguarding policy and procedure as well as formal risk assessment tools. Early research studies focusing on adult safeguarding noted worries among local authorities about the under-reporting of abuse (Brown and Stein, 1998; Taylor and Dodd, 2003). There is evidence that some authorities sought to address this by standardising procedures for reporting, investigating and responding, although there was no expectation by national government at that time that authorities should do this (Brown and Stein, 1998). Unsurprisingly, local authorities in England made more concerted efforts following the publication of the *No Secrets* guidance (Department of Health, 2000). This guidance set out expectations that agencies should work together to protect vulnerable adults, with social services being given the coordinating role. A survey in 2001 of 121 local authorities found that all had created documentation relating to vulnerable adults and that most had plans to establish multi-agency management committees (Mathew et al, 2002). However, there was some divergence around how local authorities organised their responses. Authorities adopted three broad models of safeguarding practice (Graham et al, 2017). First, some authorities used centralised specialist teams to coordinate and investigate safeguarding concerns. Second, some placed specialist safeguarding workers in operational teams. Third, some viewed safeguarding as a core part of social work practice, with all social workers being trained to investigate abuse. Risk interventions were also shaped by the LGA in response to concerns about the effects of safeguarding guidance among local government representatives, professional associations and the voluntary sector. Specifically, these parties were concerned that adults involved in safeguarding procedures had little control over the process, that 'increased services' or 'increased monitoring' were the most common outcomes from safeguarding plans and that service users were not given enough access to criminal or restorative justice (Ogilvie and Williams, 2010). These concerns led to the creation of several Making Safeguarding Personal toolkits aimed at promoting empowerment and positive risk taking, with local authorities introducing frameworks to balance the demands of safeguarding and personalisation in a similar vein (Manthorpe et al, 2015).

While interventions have been created to shape safeguarding practice, their implementation may not be straightforward. A research study conducted across eight local authorities by McCreadie et al (2008) found a lack of agreement among agencies and professionals about how the *No Secrets* guidance (Department of Health, 2000) should be interpreted. Workers across professional groups were unsure which adults should be considered 'vulnerable', what the term 'abuse' meant and who should have the final say in such decisions. Although they were named as the lead agency, social services departments felt unable to be too prescriptive about what other agencies should do. This led several agencies such as general practitioners, NHS trusts, independent providers and the voluntary sector to withdraw.

Early studies in England (McCreadie et al, 2008; McDonald, 2010), Wales (Ash, 2013) and Northern Ireland (Taylor, 2006) also highlighted a tendency for safeguarding procedures to be used defensively. This occurred for several reasons. Social workers often became focused on how the law applied to a case, leading them to seek the 'right' answer, even where uncertainties existed (McDonald, 2010). Health and safety legislation encouraged workers to adopt an approach which prioritised the safety of the service user above their autonomy (Taylor and McKeown, 2013). A fear of blame also led workers to use procedures such as multi-agency meetings or record keeping primarily to protect themselves from blame (McCreadie et al, 2008; Ash, 2013; Manthorpe et al, 2018). This point is made starkly by a social worker in McCreadie et al's study who said: 'just because I want to make sure this issue is reported doesn't mean we're going to do anything about it. … Just let's make sure that one worker doesn't take responsibility for somebody ending up killed in a couple of weeks' time' (McCreadie et al, 2008, p 255).

Not all research studies indicate that risk interventions lead to defensive practice. Later studies appear to indicate a shift in professional culture from one focused on defensible decision-making towards one focused on the rights of service users (Stevenson and Taylor, 2017; Cooper et al, 2018). This is illustrated by a worker in Stevenson and Taylor's study who said: 'I think the focus has been on taking positive risks, whereas before when you did risk assessments it was, "oh we have to stop this, we have to stop that", but now it's about how do we enable people to do this and keep as safe as possible' (2017, p 1946). While this quote comes from research in Northern Ireland, evaluations of the Making Safeguarding Personal initiative in England also suggest that social workers feel increased confidence in empowering service users to take positive risks (Cooper et al, 2018). Research by Robb and McCarthy (2023) focused on social workers' approaches to risk management interventions in cases of domestic abuse against adults with learning disabilities. The authors argue that in social work, risk becomes individualised, while in safeguarding cases, social workers accept responsibility for managing risks on behalf of the service user. Three key interventions are noted across the paper. These are relationship-based risk monitoring, managing risk by promoting choice and autonomy, and managing risk through process and bureaucracy. However, it is unclear whether these changes are universal. The confidence of workers appears to be dependent on agency culture. Workers are more likely to promote positive risk taking where they feel supported by their agency, and less likely to do so where a blame culture exists (Stevenson and Taylor, 2017).

Finally, let's consider how social work judgements about risk may impact on social relations. These can impact on risk decisions in several ways. Local authorities are responsible for screening and assessing safeguarding referrals, but the attitudes of the public and other professionals will affect what types of referral are made. While current research evidence on public attitudes to safeguarding is limited, some useful work has been done exploring attitudes to self-neglect. Interviews with the public show that people may be tolerant or even supportive of self-neglecting neighbours (Lauder et al, 2003; May-Chahal and Antrobus, 2012). While public attitudes to other forms of abuse and neglect are unclear, we can hypothesise that some safeguarding issues may be tolerated more readily than others.

Social relations between social workers and service users are likely to be key within adult safeguarding work. As noted, Robb and McCarthy (2023) reported that relationship-based risk monitoring was seen to be a key intervention by social workers supporting people with learning disabilities in cases of domestic abuse. A relational strategy with a person experiencing abuse, or someone who may be likely to experience abuse, allowed social workers to address risk in three ways. First, building a trusting relationship made it more likely that people who experienced abuse would disclose that abuse. Second, these relationships enabled social workers to engage service users in harm minimisation strategies. Third, good relationships enabled social workers to monitor situations through further contact with the service users.

Safeguarding practice is also affected by relationships between professionals. Research shows that professionals from different disciplines can embrace multidisciplinary working (Braye et al, 2014), although other studies have pointed to conflicts that can occur. In McCreadie et al's (2008) research, agencies' definitions of abuse and neglect were tacitly driven by professional self-interest. This came in different forms. Nursing home owners adopted a narrow definition of abuse to avoid highlighting unsafe practices in their homes. Social workers were reluctant to classify some situations as abusive on the grounds that it might damage their relationships with service users. Tensions occurred due to differing agency cultures, with some agencies being confused about how others conducted their part of safeguarding procedures. For example, one police officer stated that '[social workers] are incredibly cagey on the phone when they talk to you. ... They have to refer back to managers, they have to refer back to team leaders, and it's a totally different ethos to decision-making, much more rigid' (McCreadie et al, 2008, p 254). These misunderstandings of one another's roles had the potential to create uncertainty about how risk should be assessed and managed.

While social relations in risk management can be illustrated through conflict between professional groups, they are also illustrated by the way risk is managed within teams. Research by Warner and Gabe (2008) on social work judgements about risk in an inner-city mental health team found that worker judgements about risk were often 'gendered' – that is, they reflected bias to one gender or another. These judgements about gender were revealed in several ways. Male service users were seen as posing a higher risk to others than females, by both male and female workers. However, female workers in the study were more likely than their male counterparts to identify service users as 'high risk', and they identified more female service users as 'high risk'. Female workers were also more likely to talk about female service users being high risk because they were not fulfilling 'gender norms' – for instance, with respect to a service user's behaviour as a mother. While it appeared that the topic of gender roles was not discussed explicitly within the team, gender had an effect on how risk was managed. For example, male workers believed that they were called on more often to manage risks posed by male service users, while female workers were more likely to be allocated female service users who had been identified as 'risky'.

Conclusion

The purpose of this chapter was to set out the different ways of thinking about risk. The term 'risk' is often used in a common-sense way, but it can be interpreted in a multitude of different ways. Sociological theories of risk and uncertainty are useful in helping us to take a step back and consider why risk has become such a dominant theme within contemporary life. The chapter highlighted three central theories within the sociology of risk and uncertainty: Beck's risk society; governmentality, which is influenced by the work of Foucault; and Douglas' work on risk and blame. The chapter also set out more recent theories of risk work which highlight how professional workers use and are influenced by risk knowledge, interventions and social relations. Several arguments can be observed within the theoretical literature. It is commonly argued that contemporary risk narratives have been driven by a change in welfare policies. Under current regimes, people using social services are increasing encouraged to assess and manage risks in their own lives and to make informed choices about the services they access. Social work therefore becomes about assisting people to make choices through mechanisms such as care planning, or it is focused on the measurement and management of risk relating to those who not able to engage in this way. Where intervention is needed, risk assessment tools may be used. These tools are informed to a greater or lesser extent by statistical data that show patterns of behaviour within the population. Blame is an additional driving factor in social work, with practice increasingly being subject to audit, inquiries or media scrutiny. Such scrutiny is seen to encourage a focus on record keeping and defensive practice by practitioners.

Using the framework of risk work, I have reviewed the research literature on adult safeguarding and risk. This reveals several things about social work practice. Research on social workers' use of risk knowledge is limited. Existing research indicates that workers use probabilistic phrases (such as 'highly likely') but that their judgements are informed by professional values and social judgements rather than by statistical calculations. Interventions have been heavily informed by national safeguarding policies, but they are also shaped by individual authorities and local government organisations. While such interventions shape practice, it remains the case that safeguarding takes place within a multi-agency context, which creates ambiguities. How workers use interventions is also subject to change. Early adult safeguarding research identified that risk interventions were used defensively. Later research appears to indicate that workers are now willing to promote positive risk taking, possibly reflecting the policies of individual authorities to enable service users. Research also indicates that social relations may affect the ways risk is managed in several ways, with public attitudes towards safeguarding, professional relationships and individual team cultures all affecting practice. Current research evidence is patchy and demonstrates the need to investigate in greater depth how adult safeguarding risks are managed. The next three chapters set out the findings of my research with social workers in three local authorities in England.

Referrals and assessments

Introduction

As we saw in Chapter 2, academics from sociology, social policy and social work argue that risk has come to be a driving force within social work practice (Douglas and Wildavsky, 1982; Foucault, 1991; Beck, 1992; Webb, 2006; Kemshall, 2010). Several theories have been proposed to explain how concerns about risk affect society and social work. These theories are valuable, but it is important to understand how professionals understand and apply risk practices 'on the ground' (Horlick-Jones, 2005). Brown and Gale's (2018a, 2018b) model is a useful way to analyse how professionals work with risk in their day-to-day practice. The model encourages researchers to focus on the 'three core features of client-facing risk work – risk knowledge, interventions, social relations – the ways these relate to each other ... and the tensions which may emerge around these' (Brown and Gale, 2018a, p 2).

My examination of previous adult safeguarding research through the risk work framework in the previous chapter revealed several things. Social workers' risk knowledge is informed by law and policy, although legal terms and measures are often used subjectively (Stevenson and Taylor, 2017; Stevens et al, 2018). Law and policy also impact on social work interventions. Research prior to the introduction of the Care Act 2014 showed that several intervention models had evolved within local authorities. These included models where (a) safeguarding specialists were based in centralised teams or were specialists in locality social work teams, (b) safeguarding specialists were used where high risks were identified or where there were concerns within a locality, and (c) safeguarding was viewed as a task which should be done by all social workers (Graham et al, 2017). In addition, local authority practice has been shaped by the Making Safeguarding Personal initiative promoted by the LGA and ADASS (Cooper et al, 2016; Briggs and Cooper, 2018; Cooper et al, 2018). Research also indicates that social workers adopt a variety of positions when assessing risk and intervening, ranging from defensive practice to positive risk taking (McCreadie et al, 2008; Ash, 2013; Stevenson and Taylor, 2017; Cooper et al, 2018). Both the risk knowledge and interventions used influence social relations, with previous research highlighting tensions between professional groups and within social work teams (McCreadie et al, 2008; Warner and Gabe, 2008; Braye et al, 2014; Robb and McCarthy, 2023).

These insights provide us with a useful starting point for understanding how risk work is accomplished within adult safeguarding work. However, since most of the existing studies were completed before the introduction of the Care Act 2014, we need to focus on how risk work is done now. This chapter begins this journey by exploring how referrals and assessments were managed within the three local authorities in the study.

The legal status of the Care Act 2014 and the significance of new categories of abuse and neglect

When writing about risk work, Horlick-Jones (2005) observes that risk decisions are inherently political in that they rely on normative values about which actions are right or wrong. As we saw in Chapter 1, safeguarding law and policy has evolved, with changes in practice providing the context for the ways in which social workers have understood and worked with risk. Social workers in this study saw the Care Act 2014 as a significant milestone as it had made safeguarding a statutory duty for the first time. In this sense, the new legal criteria, particularly Section 42 of the Care Act 2014, was seen as the primary source of risk knowledge. This was seen to have encouraged professionals to make referrals to their local authority where there was a suspicion of abuse or neglect. Mike noted: "There has been an increase in the number of referrals. I think the Care Act has highlighted that [legal duty] to care providers, but the local authority has always done that anyway, has always wanted referrals to come in to us" (from interview). While Mike argued that the legal duties in the Care Act 2014 had led to an increase in referrals, he also noted that referrals had been encouraged by local authorities for some time. In other words, the law had acted to legitimise the view that concerns about adult safeguarding should lead to an assessment by the local authority.

As well as increased referrals due to safeguarding being a legal duty, the categories of abuse which had been introduced under the *Care and Support Statutory Guidance* (DHSC, 2022) were seen as a source of risk knowledge in that they had expanded the remit of adult safeguarding. For example, Claire noted that "especially since the Care Act, part of the Care Act includes hoarding now and self-neglect, we've seen, yes, we can say that we've seen a significant increase in safeguarding adult referrals for people that live in those kind of environments" (from interview).

Social workers listed hoarding, modern slavery, sexual exploitation and self-neglect as new categories of abuse. In making these observations, they were reflecting an actual shift in safeguarding guidance. None of these types of abuse had been listed in the *No Secrets* guidance (Department of Health, 2000),[1] though policies for managing self-neglect had previously been developed by some Safeguarding Adults Boards (Braye et al, 2015).

"We have got 80, 82 cases on the screening list": interventions to manage assessments

To understand how professionals engage in risk work, it is key to understand the interventions that they use (Brown and Gale, 2018a). Interventions can be understood as frameworks of practice which may emerge because of new knowledge or new policy concerns. As we saw in the previous section, the changes introduced under the Care Act 2014 were seen by social workers as giving greater weight to safeguarding practice – a view which was acknowledged by other professionals. These legal changes had consequences. Rates of referral increased steeply in all local authorities in line with national trends (NHS Digital, 2022). The manager in Fosborough reported that the authority received over a hundred safeguarding referrals per week. While not offering specific figures, managers in the other two authorities also indicated that their referral levels had increased year on year. As we saw in the previous chapter, local authorities have introduced a range of policies and procedures that shape interventions within safeguarding practice (Graham et al, 2017). From a risk work perspective, these can be understood as interventions. In the next section, I show that each of the three local authorities set up processes which shaped interventions and examine how social workers interpreted these processes.

To recap from the Introduction, the legal criteria for a safeguarding enquiry is set out under Section 42(1) of the Care Act 2014; this requires the local authority to consider whether there is a reasonable cause to suspect that an adult:

(a) has needs for care and support ...
(b) is experiencing, or is at risk of, abuse or neglect, and
(c) as a result of those needs is unable to protect himself or herself against the abuse or neglect or the risk of it.

This legal criteria was used by social workers as the primary source of risk knowledge, since the way decisions proceeded were based on judgements as to whether the legal criteria were met. There were some commonalities in the interventions that local authorities used in response to this knowledge. Safeguarding referrals were submitted online or by telephone, and these were screened by an initial referral teams, made up of unqualified workers. These teams also screened other types of referral for the local authority and provided information to people with care needs and their carers. The initial referral team put any safeguarding referrals through to a dedicated inbox. This task was important as it created a process by which referrals were put into the computer system. A further intervention took place in which referrals were screened by social workers, senior practitioners and team managers. These initial assessments were understood as a first step, rough and ready in nature. In other words, social workers were expected to use their judgement to decide whether there were grounds that a referral *might* reach the legal criteria. Social workers undertaking this task understood that they had to work fast to keep on top of referrals. For example, Ram, a senior practitioner in Gainsborough, told me:

> 'Today, we have got 80, 82 cases on the screening list. ... We are not able to go in depth. So, if we think a patient is vulnerable [and] that [there] is some kind of ongoing concern of risk ... then we may think this needs to be looked at further, and therefore the strategies for a risk assessment will be required. And if that's the case, it will be given to a duty worker.' (From interview)

When first observing Claire, a senior practitioner in Fosborough, I noted that "[she] works through referrals very rapidly. However, this does appear to be done thoroughly" (from field notes). I also noted down details from the referrals that she screened along with the reasons given for putting them through for further assessment or rejecting them. The following excerpts from my field notes provide some examples.

> 'Police referral regarding woman with dementia. [She was] very confused. Police concerned regarding wandering. Not viewed as safeguarding as no abuse or neglect identified. Hospital social workers copied in.'

> 'Referral by carer [care worker, based at a care home] identifying woman admitted from care home to hospital with grade 3 pressure sores. Identified as safeguarding and put through to inbox.'

> 'Medication error case. Staff member [at a care home] forgot to give medication [to a resident]. Medication not seen as life or death. [Claire] writes to home to advise [them] to follow [their] own missed med[ication]s policy.'

> 'Referral from [care] home. Notes one resident has hit another over the head with a lampshade. No injuries. Worker [Claire] identifies [she] could report [the incident] to [the] police but [it] would not be proportionate. [Claire] will put [it] through as a low priority assessment.'

These examples show that the key purpose of initial assessments was to decide whether there was evidence that criteria under Section 42(1) of the Care Act 2014 looked likely to be met and to identify the level of priority.

Cases were immediately screened out where an individual did not have an obvious care and support need, and other agencies were copied in where further action was needed which did not meet the criteria for safeguarding. To make such judgements, workers used the referral information and might also speak to referrers or other professionals. Social workers who were conducting initial assessments rarely spoke to service users, because this would disrupt the process and slow it down; cases that did require a social worker were passed on to the duty social worker in the safeguarding team. Cultural factors within teams also affected these decisions (discussed later in the chapter).

The local authorities used two different models, which affected the way social workers managed assessments and safeguarding work (see Table 2). In Fosborough, the local authority used a centralised specialist safeguarding team to conduct initial assessments and short-term safeguarding work once cases were received from the initial referral teams. This work would be conducted by social workers who were office based. Where assessments and plans could be conducted remotely, the Fosborough safeguarding team would undertake the work (or delegate it to others, such as a social worker or health worker already engaged with the person or a care home). In cases where the work was viewed as more complex, the case would be referred to the adult community teams. This arrangement caused a certain amount of tension between the safeguarding team and the adult community team. The point at which referrals should change from one team to another had altered over time, as noted by Alice, a social worker in the safeguarding team in Fosborough:

'Different messages have been given to the safeguarding team over the time they've been working. At times, they have been told they are putting too many cases through to [adult] community teams, but other times they've been told they are not putting through enough. ... People have got a lot to say about the safeguarding team and the decisions that are made, or how far the work goes to the safeguarding team, how much work they do, at what point they stop [initial assessments and longer-term assessments] and actually pass it over to the team. It's quite, kind of – what's the word – scrutinised.' (From interview)

Workers in the Fosborough safeguarding team were highly aware of the debates among managers and social workers as to the 'right' balance of referrals. This was seen as a sensitive issue as it had implications for the social relations between teams. Members of adult community teams objected to receiving referrals which they thought the safeguarding teams should have either rejected or assessed themselves. Safeguarding teams worried that

Table 2: The organisation of safeguarding in each local authority

Local authority	Initial screening	Initial assessment and short-term safeguarding work	Long-term safeguarding work
Fosborough	Initial referral team	Safeguarding team	Adult community teams
Gainsborough	Initial referral team	Safeguarding team	Safeguarding team in conjunction with adult community teams
Almsbury	Initial referral team	Safeguarding team	Safeguarding team in conjunction with adult community teams

workers in adult community teams might not see the risks they did and might, therefore, close a case because they were receiving it prematurely. Within the guidance, it is stated that workers should use 'the least intrusive response appropriate to the risk presented' (DHSC, 2022, para 14.13). When workers in the safeguarding team spoke about referrals, they generally used the term 'proportionate' as a justification for rejecting a referral to highlight that they were not making an excessive number of referrals to the adult community teams. In this sense, social workers in the safeguarding team positioned themselves primarily as a service designed to deal with acute problems, with adult community teams being responsible for longer-term work.

In Gainsborough and Almsbury, a different intervention was adopted. In these local authorities, duty workers from the safeguarding teams would screen assessments received from the initial referral teams. Members of the safeguarding teams would conduct the assessments, although they would work jointly with adult community teams. Where a case was open to a worker in a adult community team, the duty worker might ask that worker to speak to the service user about risks and how they would like them to be managed. In effect, this would mean that the safeguarding team and the member of a adult community team would co-work the case. In this arrangement, staff in the safeguarding teams gave social workers a lot of direction. For example, social workers in Almsbury gave the social workers in the adult community team a list of questions to guide conversations between them and the service user. Some of the questions were drawn from a standard template held by the safeguarding team. For example, when dealing with care home and nursing care providers, the local authority had a list of questions for referrals relating to falls, unexplained injuries, resident-on-resident physical assaults and medication errors. Once this work was complete, senior practitioners from the safeguarding team would chair safeguarding adults meetings where judged necessary. By operating in this way, social workers in the Almsbury safeguarding team positioned themselves as experts having a mentoring role for less experienced colleagues in adult community teams.

"The computer system's appalling": social workers' views on using computer systems to document referrals

When exploring how risk work is conducted, it is important to consider what forms of risk knowledge workers draw on. As Horlick-Jones notes, because the concept of risk is contested, several types of knowledge or risk framings may be used by professionals, and these may act in tension to one another (see Alaszewski, 2018). In this section, I focus on information and communications technology (ICT) systems, which are used as a source of knowledge and affect the way in which interventions are structured. Referral information was entered onto these systems by the initial referral team and safeguarding teams and adults community teams would then add to this.

ICT can be understood as 'electronic tools used to convey, manipulate and store information' (Perron et al, 2010, p 67). These systems were important because they were used to inform referrals and shaped how decisions were recorded and what actions were taken. As I explained in Chapter 2, Castel (1991) predicted that professionals would come to use risk knowledge collated and managed centrally to identify those at greatest risk within a community, with other professionals then conducting face-to-face work to confirm or disconfirm those risks. Risk assessments need to be informed by reliable information, and the advent of computer systems made it possible for large amounts of information to be recorded and easily retrieved (Petersen, 2002). In comparison to paper records, the use of ICT systems in social services allows for a greater scale of information to be retrieved and analysed. While the information is be related to the case in question, it may also be used to identify algorithms, which can be understood as sets of rules used by computers to solve specific problems (Parton, 2008). For example, safeguarding information recorded about one service user might be entered into a computer system so that it can inform future safeguarding decisions about the same or different service users. This might be achieved through computer programs which raise an alert where a certain number of concerns are highlighted about a care provider. Furthermore, safeguarding data collected at national level can be used to inform service development either locally or nationally. On the one hand, it has been argued that these changes improve safeguarding practice, in that safeguarding data can be monitored leading to better understandings of risk and 'what works' (Fyson, 2015). On the other hand, it has been seen that they lead to an audit culture in which greater focus on specific risks identified by policy makers or agencies has reduced professional discretion and acts to depersonalise practice (Webb, 2006; Parton, 2008; Rogowski, 2011; Harris, 2022).

ICT systems affected the way in which social workers did risk work in two ways. The systems were used to record knowledge about cases which could be used to inform later work. Social workers did not object to the use of ICT systems in principle, but it was common for them to question their reliability and efficiency. This view is illustrated in the following excerpt from an interview with a social worker in a adult community team in Fosborough:

Louise: The computer system's appalling, especially the safeguarding forms on it are terrible, and it's really difficult to find information, so I sometimes really struggle to find the information I need to read about safeguarding referrals and ...

Jeremy: Yes, and what's bad about them do you think?

Louise: So, it's difficult to explain really without showing you, but like sometimes you click on the safeguarding enquiry or the case notes or something and the information's just not there. There are some forms that are completely blank. I think there's historical information that I don't seem to ever be able to find − it seems like it hasn't been copied over from the previous system −and then the information you get seems to be different depending on which bit you click on the form, and just basically it's totally not user-friendly. It's really hard to find information. I have to faff about for ages trying to find the information a lot of the time, and then when I do, the safeguarding forms, a lot of what's written is just yes or no answers to questions, and there's often not really much context and much − and not much information about who [the] safeguarding team have phoned, what they've done to investigate. I don't even know whether they do much investigation in a lot of the cases, because it's really not clear. So that's all quite unhelpful.

The view put forward by Louise was typical of social workers' views across teams. ICT systems were seen to be difficult to navigate, with social workers having to access information from several different systems simultaneously. Due to the inefficiency of the ICT systems, workers adopted approaches to supplement them. For example, it was common for social workers in Gainsborough to rely on paper lists to organise and make sense of information. Nicola, a senior practitioner in Gainsborough, informed me that there were "a lot of lists" in that authority (from notes). This was not an overstatement. In addition to using the safeguarding referral screen and running records systems (using ICT systems), social workers also kept a paper task list (recording dates when the referral had been made and allocated) and a further paper cases list for handover meetings. Several workers also kept further reminders or prompts on paper. This was justified on the basis that the ICT systems were not sophisticated enough to deal with the level of referrals. For example, Nicola told me that Gainsborough's ICT system had been useful for viewing up to 10 referrals a day, but that it was impossible to make sense of larger referral numbers because the information was displayed over multiple screens, which made it difficult to read important information.

Other social workers expressed indifference to the risk knowledge generated by ICT systems. Margaret commented that data from cases would lead to risk knowledge at national level. She said:

'You know, obviously the information we get is useful for us, but it is also feeding in to some government statistics, isn't it? So, we have to have that information. So, yes, sometimes you think why do I do that? But that is because the government are keeping information on how many of this, and how many of that and whatever. I don't worry too much about it. I just fill out the forms.' (From interview)

Margaret's account highlights the expectation that local authorities will collect standard data on safeguarding adult cases. This data has both local and national roles: it is used by Safeguarding Adults Boards to self-evaluate their performance; and it feeds into the Safeguarding Adults Collection data collated by the NHS (SCIE, 2016; NHS Digital, 2022). While Margaret acknowledged that such data had an audit function, her comment that she just filled out the forms signalled a disconnection from the process. Comments like this were typical of several social workers in the study who acknowledged processes of central oversight but appeared indifferent to them.

ICT systems were used to record risk knowledge, which social workers and other professionals could draw from. However, the systems were also used to organise and shape social work interventions. Members of safeguarding teams in all local authorities used screens which displayed the incoming referrals on graphs. When looking at the computer screens, the workers were faced with a large number of boxes, including service user names and other details. These boxes were colour coded to indicate how urgent the assessments were. During my first day in Gainsborough, I recorded the following example:

'referral [is opened by Mike] – 89 referrals [are shown] when opening up [the] screen. [The] referrals [are] in boxes [which] are colour coded. The majority are red, the odd one or two orange and a few green. The number of red boxes seems quite overwhelming. [An] explanation [is given to me by Mike], "Red – The initial referral team will have told us it is urgent. Orange – [the risk is] not insignificant [and we] need to make a phone call to query if [there is an] incident to look at. Green – [is] general information [or a] request for assessment.'" (From field notes)

When speaking to Nicola about the same system, I was told: "You get used to it. If the greens aren't screened out, it feels unresponsive. However higher priority work also needs doing, so it is difficult to clear" (From field notes).

To me, the numbers of cases on the system always seemed alarming, with the reds seeming to spotlight a high degree of danger which the workers were expected to navigate. The number of referrals did frame practice in that workers felt the need to keep on top of the referral system and ensure that the numbers remained manageable. However, there were times when social workers chose to use their own discretion to change the ways in which they intervened. Mike said: "When safeguarding gets too stressful, we'll pick off a few greens. If greens are left too long, they become reds or more urgent" (From field notes). Thus, questioning the logic of the risk knowledge on the ICT system enabled social workers to take on a variety of referrals. This type of discretion was sanctioned by senior practitioners in teams and served to reduce stress and enable workers to engage in preventative work.

Previous research has shown that interventions using ICT systems can blunt social workers' compassion. In his ethnography of hospital social work practice, Burrows (2020) describes a computer screen that highlighted which patients were medically fit for discharge through colour coding according to level of priority. He writes, "the computer screen and its colour coding has a dehumanising effect on the construction of the patient, who is reduced to a unit who must be shifted, rather than a person with unique needs and a unique history" (2020, p 65). In other words, the use of ICT systems presents risk knowledge about service users in an abstract way, which reduces worker empathy and increases management control over workers. This was evident in some cases where ICT systems were used as the sole source of information with little discretion applied. For example, Claire screened the following referral:

'Police report. Male 1 stated that he wanted to kill Male 2 and make him suffer. Male 1 told police he had unstable PD [personality disorder]. Police believed [the] threat [was] significant. Male 2 stated he wanted to jump off [a] balcony following this. Assessed as not safeguarding on the grounds that Male 2 had no documented care and support needs which would lead him to be unable to protect himself. Email to police to confirm [the case was] not safeguarding.' (From field notes)

In this case, the computer system was used to verify that the client (Male 1) had no record of an unstable personality disorder. This was then used to justify discharge. However, the discrepancy between the service user's account (telling the police he had an unstable personality disorder) and the records was not examined. These practices acted in tension to statements by social workers that the ICT systems provided incomplete information which could not be relied on without further assessment.

An further argument made within the social work literature, is that computers are used by managers to create certain types of risk knowledge which heavily shape the actions of workers (Parton, 2008). This point was acknowledged by social workers, although they did not always object to it. For example, Mike said:

> 'there is quite tight protocols around how long it should take to do the different stages, and if there is a delay in that, that is recorded, why there has been a delay, and our managers and her manager will pick up on those things. It does get noticed through the documents that we produce following meetings and through the monitoring of the computer system as well. They will be able to see how long it has taken from when a referral is received to when it is allocated, for example. I think there is a thoroughness in what is done as well as it being timely.' (From interview)

In this quote, the "monitoring of the computer system" was seen to provide an audit trail which tracked when meetings occurred and how they were recorded. Rather than being seen as form of oppressive control, this process was praised because it ensured that processes were thorough and allowed for missed cases to be spotted.

Building a picture: assessing safeguarding risks

In their review of the risk work literature, Gale et al (2016) argue that a central component to risk work is translating risks. Professionals are encouraged to use institutionally sanctioned modes of knowledge to make risk decisions. However, they may also be faced with problems of 'ecological fallacy' in which the risk knowledge they are encouraged to use is not useful or cannot easily be tested in their day-to-day practice (Heyman et al, 2013). This provides practitioners with a moral dilemma as they are forced to decide which type of risk knowledge is most relevant. Social workers conducting safeguarding enquiries drew on records from the ICT systems, but this type of knowledge was seen as incomplete and piecemeal. Social workers had to trawl through referral systems and case records to find out whether there had been previous allegations of abuse and to identify the current situation. Consequently, social workers stressed that they needed to do further assessment to make sense of the pieces and create contextualised risk knowledge about the person. This process was described as an expectation by several workers. For example, Simon stated, "part of my report is summarising all previous safeguarding" (from interview). This process was described in more detail by Alice, in Fosborough, who described her thinking in relation to one case. She said:

> 'so you are reading through, you are taking in the information to build up the picture, but I think when you are on the safeguarding team, you are quite sort of focused on working out is it or isn't it safeguarding? But it was clear, I mean I think it was like looking, as far as I can remember, back at the other referrals and seeing the full picture and that made me think there is definitely a problem here. It sort of built the picture.' (From interview)

As noted by Alice, when assessing safeguarding referrals, social workers looked for information which would help them to judge whether the legal criteria for safeguarding was met. For Alice, the case in question related to concerns about an older adult being neglected by her son, who was acting as carer. While Alice had not completed the safeguarding assessment, she identified several factors which rang alarm bells and prompted her to pass the case on to an adult community team for a fuller assessment. The alarm bells were reports of arguments between the mother and son, reports that the son was experiencing mental health problems, allegations that the son was taking money from his mother without consent and concern that the mother lacked capacity to make decisions relating to her care. While none of these had been substantiated at the time of the observation, the culminative picture prompted the worker to arrange a more detailed assessment.

When making an assessment, social workers had to weigh the knowledge gained from their assessment (drawing on the knowledge from the ICT systems) against their knowledge of the Care Act 2014. As has been noted in legal research, such judgements are never impartial, but rather are informed by ethical considerations or the values of the worker (Abbott, 2022). At the point where duty social workers in each authority picked up the case, it had been subject to an initial assessment. However, the initial assessment process was viewed as necessarily quick and dirty, meaning that a further process of assessment needed to take place. When making judgements about whether the case fitted the statutory criteria, social workers first referred to Section 42 of the Care Act 2014. While this section was seen to offer the key criteria, several social workers indicated that they struggled to apply it to cases because it was not specific enough. For example, Rachel said,

"When you look at Section 42, it seems a bit woolly" (from interview). As already mentioned, social workers used the *Care and Support Statutory Guidance* (DHSC, 2022) to identify which types of abuse and neglect should be considered as adult safeguarding issues. The categories of abuse provided in this guidance are intended to be examples, with the guidance stating that '[l]ocal authorities should not limit their view of what constitutes abuse or neglect' (DHSC, 2022, para 14.17). Nonetheless, most social workers used the categories listed as a way of identifying what type of risk they were looking at and the tools they might use to assess it. In line with social workers in Ash's (2013) study, many social workers felt more confident where there were set assessment questions to guide them. Some local authorities had created lists of questions in relation to categories of abuse introduced for the first time under the *Care and Support Statutory Guidance* in 2014 (DHSC, 2022). These lists were welcomed by workers. For example, Rachel identified that the guidance relating to self-neglect and hoarding was helpful "because there are bullet points to guide you" (from interview). However, she and other workers complained that other categories of abuse had no tools, which made the assessment processes more difficult.

Although some workers welcomed local policies or tools which aided them in translating risks, such mechanisms were not appreciated in all circumstances. Alice informed me that the assessment processes in Fosborough was guided by tools purchased by the local authority from an independent company. Giving a wry laugh, she showed me the logo on one of the documents, which said, "we solve complex social problems by changing behaviours". Alice told me the organisation had recommended that social workers should avoid using the word 'need', as it was dependency creating. While they were supportive of the notion of strengths-based practice (Saleeby, 2013), team members felt that the main intent behind the new assessment tools was cost-cutting. Certain questions and prompts suggested by the company, such as "tell me about a time when you were happy in your life", were deemed insensitive within the context of safeguarding. In response, the Fosborough safeguarding team wrote their own assessment questions, incorporating some of the questions suggested by the commissioned company but omitting or rephrasing others.

Professional judgement and team cultures

Not all risk knowledge is provided through law and policy or through agency procedures. Professional judgement or team cultures may also drive the way risk is assessed by professional groups and how they intervene (Brown and Calnan, 2012). Observations of social workers revealed that they were using two processes when deciding how to intervene.

First, when judging whether individuals with care and support needs met the criteria for a safeguarding enquiry, workers needed to decide whether the risk of harm was significant. A first consideration was the severity of the risk, which was informed by social workers' professional judgement. For example, Nicola spoke of a case where a service user with a physical disability had contacted to a drop-in centre to report abuse. When recalling the case, she noted:

> 'he was saying he didn't want to go home, because he had been assaulted by his brother and he was scared, and he was saying right there and then. So he had rung, well she [the drop-in worker] had obviously rung the customer service desk and they had spoken to me, so even before we got that onto the system, I thought actually, we need to do something about that. So there's an opportunity to, because we are very process led, but actually you use your social worker head and think, right, this needs a response. We can get the IT stuff done afterwards; actually I need to work out where he is and I need to get a social worker out to go and see him and we need to look if we can find some alternative accommodation if that's what he wants.' (From interview)

In this case, the severity of the risk was judged to require immediate action. Nicola's comment that she had to use her "social worker head" signalled that the level of risk required a professional decision on whether to act. In using this phrase, she identified that she was drawing on a set of professional values to override the procedures of the local authority, which she painted as "process led"; justifications for the intervention could be thought through after action had been taken. These findings align with Burrows' (2020) study on hospital social workers, which found that social workers felt an ultimate loyalty to the service user rather than to their employer or the health authority.

The second process involved social workers looking for patterns or risk within referral information. For example, Mavis was working with a case in which an older adult was reported to have had a serious fall in a care home. Staff at the home claimed that the fall had been an accident. However, Mavis was sceptical of this explanation and set out to assess whether the home had been negligent. To achieve this, she looked for patterns within the data. She said:

> 'That's what I'm looking for – to see whether there's been any other, whether there's a spike anywhere in unwitnessed falls and see if that, you know, find out from that, well, has that got anything to do with how much staffing there was at that time, what time of day it was – those sorts of things, just to try and get patterns, really.' (From interview)

The view that social workers should be looking for patterns in the data was prevalent in all three local authorities, but this activity was not informed by national or local policies. In this case, Mavis described looking for patterns in the staffing levels within the enquiry process as a way of looking at whether preventable harm had taken place. However, when examining referrals, social workers also looked for evidence of small harms over time, particularly in cases where a person was cared for by a family member, a care agency, a care home or a nursing home. The logic to this was that one or two small harms might be viewed as accidental, whereas evidence of the same harm several times over months or years might signal a pattern of abuse or neglect. Judgements about the severity of risk and patterns of risk were used by all teams. They were not written in policy and procedure, but acted as a form of professional knowledge through which social workers made decisions about the severity of risk.

A common question raised within the social work literature is the degree of agency individual social workers have. It is commonly claimed that decisions about risks and thresholds are heavily controlled through agency protocols or managerial control, giving little scope for worker autonomy (Webb, 2009; Pollack, 2010; Rogowski, 2011). The implication here is that if social workers were allowed to exercise discretion, they would do so to the benefit of the service user. The social workers I observed often reported that they imposed high risk thresholds when making judgements about whether or not cases met the criteria for a safeguarding enquiry.[2] However, rather than believing that they were influenced by formal agency protocols, they indicated that they were informed by social norms which were often agreed through team discussions or conversations. These informed decisions when judging where thresholds should lie. For example, Lisa said:

'So, I don't feel pressure, in this role I haven't had pressure from above to be more ruthless with thresholds. It's just, I suppose, you take on board what the people on the team are doing, and also I'm aware that waiting lists are very high, so you need to think about prioritising the most important cases.' (From interview)

Notably, Lisa says that she did not feel pressured by her manager, but considered what other members of the team were doing and the number of referrals on the waiting list. Lisa's concern to match her judgements with those of other social workers was typical and could be seen in my observation of others. Social workers would regularly check with peers or senior practitioners as to whether their judgements felt correct. This form of checking had the benefit of allowing social workers to see the referral through a fresh pair of eyes, but it was also driven by a team belief that there needed to be consistency in judgements. However, it was notable that such judgements were often utilitarian in nature (aiming to promote the greatest good for the greatest number) rather than focusing on the ethical rights of the individual service user.

Inappropriate referrals

When doing risk work, practitioners must draw on professional knowledge and apply this within interventions. However, this process may have impacts on their relationships with other professionals, which also needs to be considered (Brown and Gale, 2018b). A key theme within social worker accounts was that there were many 'inappropriate referrals'. These judgements drew on social workers' risk knowledge in that they were building a picture from the referral information and information on file. In framing referrals as misguided, social workers drew on their legal risk knowledge. However, they also used social relations, as they made evaluations of the motive behind the referral. Lisa described this process in the following way: "so I am looking at the intention behind the referral. What is the intention of the referrer, what is the intention of the person who suffered the injury who reported it" (From interview).

Inappropriate referrals were seen to come about because of a professional's general concern that a person had care and support needs which were not being met. A common example was cases of self-neglect. Emergency service workers would visit a property and observe someone living in poor housing conditions, and this would lead them to highlight it as a safeguarding issue. Lisa characterised these referrals as being driven by a belief that "something needs to be done" (from field notes). Although social workers viewed this as understandable, it was commonly painted as misguided, on the basis that the cases did not meet the Section 42 criteria. For example, Karen said:

> 'Well, I'd say that our health colleagues perhaps mix up concerns they have about cases with what we would call safeguarding issues. I mean, of course, you know, they flag up cases where social work input might be useful or housing might be useful, but it isn't necessarily safeguarding.' (From interview)

While health professionals were seen as being overcautious, referrals from emergency service workers were viewed with an even higher degree of scepticism. When receiving a referral from the fire service, Kerry told me: "Before I even look at this, I am going to make an assumption. This is an unhygienic cluttered house" (From field notes). The subsequent referral did indicate this, but it also identified domestic violence. Kerry's initial reaction was: "sounds to me like care and support rather than safeguarding". She then went on to look for further evidence, which indicated that the person had a learning disability, and at this point she decided that a safeguarding enquiry was needed. In taking this approach, Kerry adopted a process common among social workers: start with a hypothesis that emergency service referrals are inappropriate and then look for evidence to disprove this. While this approach might seem reasonable (as workers were making an assessment about whether the legal criteria were met), it was notable that referrals by care home managers and nursing home managers were treated differently. These workers were viewed as liable to underreport safeguarding concerns. The reasoning behind this view was that care home and nursing home staff have been encouraged to self-report accidents or abuse in their own establishments. This led social workers to assess whether the referred risk was an honest one, with social workers commonly voicing suspicions that they might be playing down the severity of the risk. The issue of how abuse and neglect in care homes were assessed and managed is dealt with in more depth in Chapter 5.

In addition to believing that inappropriate referrals came about because of well-intentioned but misguided concerns of other professionals, social workers identified that inappropriate referrals were made due to 'defensive practice'. In making this argument, their views aligned with Douglas (1992) in that they accepted that notions of risk are associated with censure or blame. Patricia spoke of this dynamic in relation to referrals from care homes:

'I think providers are really worried about any repercussions, because it is better for them because once they have referred, it's a weight off their shoulders, which I understand, you know, I totally understand that. And we will berate them if they don't. This [is] the problem.' (From interview)

Patricia's mention of making a referral as leading to a "weight off" referrers' shoulders painted a picture in which making a referral might mitigate responsibility for the risk. Her comment that "we will berate them if they don't" also acknowledged that the local authority could be seen to be giving out mixed messages on the reporting of safeguarding risks.

While Patricia's statement was made in relation to care home staff, this dynamic was seen to operate more widely. Press reports highlighting abuse and neglect and the safeguarding adults reviews which followed them were seen to have brought about an expectation that professionals should refer abuse or neglect where they saw it. National and local events were regarded as significant in raising people's concern about blame. Adrian referred to the Grenfell Tower tragedy in London having an impact on referrals related to fire risks. The Grenfell Tower fire, which killed 72 residents in 2017, was widely reported in the national press (MacLeod, 2018), with the subsequent inquiry criticising the Royal Borough of Kensington and Chelsea for the 'political neglect' of its poorer residents (Independent Grenfell Recovery Taskforce, 2017, p 4). In his interview, Adrian spoke about a referral he had received relating to a man with mental health needs. Adrian noted that there were concerns the resident might be tampering with electrical wires in a way that constituted "quite a mild fire risk". In describing the fire risk as "mild", he cast doubt on the seriousness of the risk presented in the referral. However, he acknowledged that his response to the referral had been influenced by the Grenfell tragedy. He said:

> 'So we're post-Grenfell Tower now. ... And, you know, and its, the fire risk thing is coming a lot. There are a lot more fire risk referrals it seems, or ... there's a lot more attention to that in big, multi-occupancy blocks ... I think, yes, just on the grapevine, yes, it seems like that's ... people are saying that it's a bigger thing. Housing are saying it, you know, it's in discussions particularly about this case with the housing officer. They're like, yes, we're being asked to pay attention to this issue.' (From interview)

Renewed public anxiety in multiple-occupancy flats was seen as a precursor to the referral, with Adrian stating that several professionals had made "a concerted [effort] to kind of push it through, you know, through the point, you know, [that] demonstrated that he'd met the threshold for a Section 42 enquiry" (from interview).

The level of public anxiety about fire risks had an influence not only on the level of referrals but also on the way local authorities assessed them. Adrian's account indicated that other workers were determined to make a group effort to ensure that local authorities assessed certain cases as a safeguarding concern. In some cases, these coordinated responses were seen to be driven by a perception among professionals that "we [the local authority] fob them off and we don't take them seriously" (Adrian, from interview). Workers indicated that they might not always accept that the risks suggested by other professionals were valid. However, the national context motivated them to conduct thorough assessments prior to forming this view, and they ensured that the rationale for their decisions were carefully documented.

In some cases, social workers voiced suspicion that professionals were making a safeguarding referral to 'game the system'. For example, Claire told me that "referrers come to the safeguarding team [rather than to adult community teams for a Care Act assessment] due to our quick response time" (from field notes). In a similar vein, social workers believed that where there was a long waiting list for Care Act assessments, referrers tried to push cases forward by presenting them as safeguarding concerns. As an observer in the office, it was difficult for me to judge whether such concerns were justified.

However, while such referrals were disapproved of, social workers were still observed using tact in their interactions with colleagues. Commonly, social workers balanced risk judgement and social relations by identifying why the criteria for interventions were met and, where care needs were evident, identifying alternative care pathways. Across these decisions, social workers saw themselves as the arbiter of judgements about risk and, in doing so, highlighted their own professional authority.

Discouraging or encouraging referrals?

Decisions about risk are affected by social relations between professionals managing risk and other parties (Brown and Gale, 2018b). These social relationships may be positively or negatively affected by the way judgements and decisions about risk are communicated. Most social workers were of the view that a high proportion of safeguarding referrals did not meet the criteria for a safeguarding enquiry. Social workers voiced two contrasting views on interventions which should be used to shape future practices. Both of these relied on building social relations with other professionals. On the one hand, several participants identified the need to educate referrers about which risks should be viewed as significant. This view was illustrated by Rebecca who said, "[we should] also be open and educate the public and go out to nursing homes and share good practice and kind of give feedback about the referrals we receive to care providers etcetera" (From interview). Similarly, Margaret, a manager in Fosborough, said, "so I am really trying hard to develop relationships with people so that we understand what they do and they understand what we do" (From interview). This approach was prompted by a view that professionals outside of social work generally had a poor understanding of the Care Act 2014. Some managers and senior practitioners argued that if those making referrals understood the legal criteria better, they would be less likely to make referrals which did not meet the Section 42 criteria. This approach had been used in all three local authorities, with managers recognising that other professionals might also make suggestions which would improve local referral processes.

On the other hand, some spoke of the need to encourage referrals. This view was made on the basis that to recognise abuse or mistreatment, small incidences of abuse and neglect needed to be recorded so that patterns of risk can be spotted over time. In line with this way of thinking, the computer system in Fosborough allowed safeguarding concerns which did not meet the criteria for a safeguarding enquiry to be 'badged' to make it easier for workers to spot patterns if subsequent referrals were made. This view that referrals need to be encouraged was illustrated by Mike, who stated:

'we want to hear if there is a concern and that it is not necessarily an admission of fault or that somebody is to blame for what has happened, but it may just be that there has been an accident or something has happened that we need to be made aware of.' (From interview)

From this perspective, reporting was seen to be useful in that it could lead the way to preventive work. However, this approach was seen by some workers as having limits, in that it was seen to encourage defensive practice which then clogged up the referrals system. For example, Nicola said:

'I think that's probably the history behind that and, of course, it's good to get patterns, but the other side of that is you do have people ringing in. I mean I think providers now, and we get all sorts of phone calls ... the initial referral ... [team members] say, you know, someone's, I don't know, tapped someone ever so slightly on the hand – is that safeguarding? No, it's not. So, I think we've maybe become a bit scared really.' (From interview)

Social workers mainly supported one approach or the other when dealing with other professionals, although in some cases, as seen in Nicola's comment, they acknowledged that obtaining patterns from the data was useful but that encouraging referrals had gone too far. However, the tension between the two approaches was rarely raised explicitly among team members and so remained an open issue.

Conclusion

This chapter, which has focused on referrals and assessments, reveals several new findings about the way in which risk work has been conducted by social workers involved with adult safeguarding. In line with previous research, safeguarding law and policy was central to the knowledge social workers used when identifying whether a risk was present (Stevenson and Taylor, 2017; Stevens et al, 2018). The Care Act 2014 (particularly Section 42) and the *Care and Support Statutory Guidance* (DHSC, 2022) were used to identify whether a person's circumstances should be viewed as a safeguarding risk or as a care need more generally. Social workers across the local authorities indicated that the Care Act 2014 had increased the status of safeguarding, with the directives and guidance taken more seriously by health and social care professionals than the previous *No Secrets* guidance (Department of Health, 2000).

The three local authorities in the study used two intervention models which differed from those identified previously (Graham et al, 2017). Fosborough adopted a model in which initial screening was conducted by unqualified workers in an initial referral team. Initial assessments and short-term safeguarding work was then conducted by a safeguarding team with long-term work being referred to an adult community team, who were responsible for long-term case work more generally. In contrast, Gainsborough and Almsbury adopted a model in which initial screening was conducted by unqualified workers in an initial referral team, and initial assessments and short-term safeguarding work was conducted by a safeguarding team. Long-term safeguarding work was conducted jointly by the safeguarding team and adult community teams. Tensions were evident in the social relations between social workers in the Fosborough safeguarding team and the adult community teams, where there were ongoing debates about the 'right number of referrals' from one team to another. Social relations between social workers in the safeguarding teams and adult community teams were less fraught in Gainsborough and Almsbury, as greater guidance and mentoring was given by social workers in safeguarding teams.

ICT systems acted as a key source of knowledge for social workers when assessing and managing safeguarding risks. However, the logics of the ICT systems did not drive risk assessment and management in reductive ways, as previously suggested (Webb, 2006; Parton, 2008; Rogowski, 2011). Social workers either felt that ICT systems had the potential to provide a useful form of knowledge or they were indifferent to the systems. However, the ICT systems on offer were difficult to navigate, glitchy and sometimes had important information missing. This meant that they were propped up or supplemented by systems informally designed by teams or individual workers. As well as being a source of knowledge, ICT systems shaped interventions by indicating which assessments were urgent. While social workers used these systems generally, they also exercised discretion and assessed some less urgent cases, both to prevent such cases escalating and to manage the stress of risk work. Safeguarding assessments were seen as a process of building a picture. These interventions involved social workers drawing on existing risk information and identifying gaps which needed to be filled through further assessment work.

While legal and policy knowledge was used to guide decisions as to whether people who had been referred to safeguarding met the criteria, social workers also drew on other forms of knowledge when deciding how to act. Professional values were used at times to override the process-led models of the local authority. In addition, social workers were guided by team culture – for instance, the expectation that social workers should be searching for patterns of abuse within case histories over time. Constant discussion within teams was also used to provide consistency in decisions about whether the safeguarding criteria had been met.

Safeguarding referrals were received from a wide range of agencies. Many of these referrals were judged to be inappropriate. Social relations were central to decisions about how to intervene, with social workers aiming to assess the intentions behind referrals. Social work interventions in relation to the referral were, then, shaped by judgements as to whether the referral had been made due to concerns about the general welfare of the person, concerns about blame or more cynical attempts to 'game the system'. The difficulty of conducting risk work in the context of ever-increasing referrals led to debates about whether the local authority should be encouraging or discouraging referrals. There was disagreement among social workers on this point, indicating that individual workers differed in how they managed social relations with referrers.

Personalised safeguarding: policy, principles and practice realities

Introduction

Chapter 3 identified how safeguarding referrals and assessments were managed within the three local authorities. It established several aspects of the conduct of risk work within adult safeguarding. Knowledge of the legal and policy framework was seen as central to safeguarding practice, although this knowledge was viewed as somewhat ambiguous at times. Risk knowledge was also provided through ICT systems, although this was seen as partial and somewhat difficult to access. Interventions were shaped through agency models of practice. Differences were noted between Fosborough, which opted to conduct short-term safeguarding work remotely by telephone and using online formats, and the other local authorities, in which safeguarding teams and adult community teams had a closer relationship. The ICT systems played a central role in interventions across all local authorities, allowing social workers to identify priority cases. However, the information on these systems was viewed as partial, with the assessment process being viewed as one in which social workers brought existing information together and established where further information was required. Professional decision-making and cultural knowledge within teams informed this process. Social relations were core to the assessment process, with social workers aiming to assess the intentions of people making referrals. As Chapter 3 identified that law and policy was a central part of risk, knowledge, this chapter zooms in on how social workers understood this.

Historically speaking: Social workers' perceptions of law and policy changes

In the previous chapter, I identified how the Care Act 2014 was central to social workers' knowledge when conducting risk work. This was evident in social workers' screening and assessment work, in which they referenced the Care Act 2014, statutory guidance and local policy while also drawing on professional decision-making and team culture. Risk work theorists note that although practitioners draw on forms of knowledge, they may also question it (Brown and Gale, 2018a). Such questioning was notable in the accounts of social workers in my study. They did not just accept current law and policy, but sought to understand the changes which had occurred over time. Their accounts focused on the importance of including service user wishes. For example, Marcia stated:

'when I first started doing the safeguarding work, it wasn't really like that, where you ... with the person at the centre of it, you are involving them. It was more about people making decisions outside of the person, as to what they feel they should, you know, they should be doing or what the actions should be. Whereas now it really is focused on putting the person at the heart of it and saying "what do you want?" if they've got the capacity to make the decision – supporting them to make the decision for themselves. And involving them in all of your decision-making and all of your actions.' (From interview)

Participants saw the Making Safeguarding Personal initiative as key to a shift in the social work knowledge base, with the values being reflected in the Care Act 2014. This is illustrated in an excerpt from my interview with Simon:

Simon: And I think, traditionally, social workers think that they do it to somebody.
Jeremy: Yes.
Simon: There's ... which is not good.
Jeremy: Hmm.
Simon: It's a bit like whatever pressure that person's feeling, we'll go in and we try and, you know, I suppose being quite paternalistic, really.
Jeremy: Hmm.
Simon: But this, the Care Act, is definitely pointing towards person-centred safeguarding, and it's about giving power to the person. Just saying we're here to help you, you know, work out what you want to do and we will try and support you in fulfilling your wishes on what you want ...
Jeremy: Hmm.
Simon: ... how you want to resolve this. We'll help you to explore what the options are and what you can and ...
Jeremy: Yes.
Simon: ... but it's up to you. It's putting the power to that person.

Marcia and Simon both reflected a common view among social workers that Making Safeguarding Personal and the Care Act 2014 represented a positive shift in ideology away from paternalism and towards empowerment. This change in the knowledge framework then changed the types of interventions which might be offered and signalled more positive social relations with service users. As I note in Chapter 2, personalisation policies have been criticised by academics on the basis that they promote individualisation, in which the management of risk is transferred from the state to the individual (Scourfield, 2007; Ferguson, 2012). These critiques were absent from social workers' accounts when they were discussing policy changes; instead, individuals were supportive of the concepts of choice and personalisation. On one level, this is unsurprising. Journal articles are not read widely, and practitioners are often unaware of academic critiques. However, it was surprising that practitioners quite readily accepted the view that social workers had acted paternalistically in the past, particularly as some of them would have been practising within this period. Nonetheless, changes to law and policy were seen as having had a positive influence on the profession's knowledge in relation to managing risk.

Austerity and resources

As Brown and Gale (2018b) note, theoretical ideas about risk cannot always be applied smoothly to real-world situations. This may lead practitioners to question the truth of existing risk knowledge, the legitimacy of interventions or their impact on social relations (where the authenticity of experiences and interactional practices is questioned). As we have seen, interpreting law and policy is a central component in the risk work of social workers engaged in adult safeguarding. As the social workers in my research viewed safeguarding law and policy positively, they did not question the truth of risk knowledge. However, the legitimacy of risk interventions in the existing financial circumstances and their impact on social relations (with service users and other professionals) were frequently questioned.

Social workers saw the resourcing of social services and health services as a major obstacle to the delivery of safeguarding interventions. The constraints on social work funding in the UK are well known. The global financial crisis in 2008 saw governments step in to ensure that banks did not fail. Austerity policies pursued in the UK by the Coalition Government in 2010–16 and by the Conservative Government from 2016 led to sharp reductions in local authority spending, and this also impacted on some voluntary organisations due to their reliance on local authority contracts (Hernandez, 2021). Sector guidance has advocated that social workers should continue to provide personalised support and that personalisation principles should be applied to safeguarding (LGA and ADASS, 2018; LGA and ADASS, 2019; LGA, 2022a). However, critics note that funding reductions threaten to undermine the ability of local authorities to provide preventative services or commission services which provide service users with choice (Lymbery, 2014).

Social workers in my study highlighted tensions between the aims of personalised safeguarding policies and the interventions that their local authority could provide in practice. For example, Alice noted the increased pressure on resources:

Alice: I just think there is a big tension between the resources we have and the practice that we can undertake in the department. I think that's the problem.

Jeremy: Has that always been the case or is it …

Alice: Well, no, I mean obviously it's got harder and harder because we were starved of funding in the council, you know?

The shortages of resources brought about by austerity were seen to impact on risk work in three ways, described next.

"The last stop": safeguarding as a service of last resort

Social workers argued that funding cuts led to higher thresholds being applied to existing care services. Because of this, more cases were referred to safeguarding. This then added to the complexity of cases being referred to safeguarding, as user needs increased while individuals remained on waiting lists to receive care. This point was made by Victoria, who said: "I think the quantity of stuff that we get has increased, but it's also the complexity of it. It takes a bit longer to kind of work through some stuff and to do it properly" (from interview).

During the period when I was observing workers in Gainsborough, social workers were having to negotiate difficult work due to a care firm (which I have named Complecare) experiencing financial difficulties. Social work managers had received notice that the company might go bust, leading to an influx of safeguarding referrals related to visits carried out by Complecare staff. Social workers described cases in which Complecare care workers who delivered domiciliary care had missed visits, left long gaps between visits or turned up several hours late. This had resulted in service users not receiving scheduled medications, not being fed or being left wearing incontinence pads for extended times. Senior local authority managers were in meetings with Complecare, but had also instructed social workers to monitor the situation on the ground. Victoria said:

'I think having some providers that, things are a lot less stable, so you know this kind of stuff with Complecare, you know, they might go under and we will have to try and find care for like a hundred and fifty people. You know, we had, a couple of months ago, quite a small care provider in the area that just went into liquidation and we had to try and help people to find other alternatives. And that was quite small, but it's still, you know, different types of work that I am not sure would have necessarily been so prevalent like ten years ago, or five years ago, and I think some of the knock, you know, the knock-on effects of other resources, other agencies being cut – NHS, mental health – I think there is a bit of a view, you know, social services kind of is the last stop. And then I think we are not always very good at saying no.' (From interview)

In this account, the financial difficulties faced by Complecare were seen as one element of welfare cuts more generally. Victoria's view of social services as the "last stop" illustrated how referrals to social services would be made when other services were being cut. In these cases, needs were being framed as safeguarding issues, although the safeguarding risks had arisen due to the lack of community services. Such dynamics were highlighted by workers across all three local authorities, and social workers were presented with dilemmas as to how such matters should be resolved regarding the safeguarding process.

Blockages in the system: the effects of reduced resources on safeguarding interventions

Lack of funding was seen as the main driver of problems within local authorities, and by extension safeguarding services, but in addition, several interventions were seen as working suboptimally. Some safeguarding duties could only be allocated to managers or senior practitioners. Amanda, a team manager in Gainsborough, said:

'So, I've got four and a half senior practitioners, and as I said to you before, they've got lots of different roles. So, they've got screening, they've got to manage duty, they've got to manage staff, they've got to authorise support plans for mainstream social work cases. They've got their informal supervision to do, and they attend things like MARAC [Domestic Abuse Multi-agency Risk Assessment Conference], same as the other senior practitioners. And they also chair, well their role is to chair the safeguarding adult meetings. Now I get involved in that quite a lot, so I do quite a lot of senior practitioner work as well, because these guys … it's just not resourced well enough, so I have to do it.' (From interview)

In line with Amanda's observation, several social workers in the study reported that senior practitioner posts were often vacant, which led to backlogs in the system. Senior managers in Gainsborough had tried to temper this problem by allowing standard-grade social workers to conduct some screening tasks. However, social workers felt that this had only a limited effect on workers' capacity in the safeguarding system, as factors such as team members' level of experience might limit the pool of social workers who could respond to a case.

While team managers in Fosborough and Gainsborough acknowledged that staffing levels were subject to fluctuation, throughput within the safeguarding system was judged by social workers to be a recurrent problem. This was particularly the case in Fosborough, where staff in the safeguarding team referred cases to adult community teams for longer-term work. Safeguarding team members reported that there had been staff shortages in their own team and in adult community teams. They noted that there could be delays of several months between their team identifying the need for a safeguarding enquiry and the adult community teams carrying it out. Social workers in the safeguarding teams did not blame workers in the adult community team for this, but they worried about the quality of work being undertaken. For example, Alice reported:

'I know there is one team, they've got virtually no social workers, and it's just like, in a way it's not fair, because the managers are having to just try to prioritise as best they can. But the thing is, like, I was doing another case recently, and the team concerned dealt with it as best they could, but actually there was a pretty big omission … somewhere along the line, because we didn't have enough input and they just dealt with things with a very long arm [and] it [allegations of abuse against care home staff] was missed.' (From interview)

As Alice's case illustrates, safeguarding team members worried about the effects of staff shortages in adult community teams. This led some social workers to hold onto safeguarding cases for long periods, despite directions from senior management that they should pass the cases to adult community teams for longer-term safeguarding work. These issues, related to the resourcing of services, led social workers to question the legitimacy of their interventions as workers were having to constantly bridge the tension between how the safeguarding system was intended to work and the resources available to them under austerity.

"I don't even pick up the phone to [care] homes anymore": the effects of austerity measures on social relations

In addition to challenging the legitimacy of interventions under current resourcing pressures, social workers highlighted ways in which social relations had been affected by austerity measures. The pressure on resources affected social workers' relationships with care providers in two ways.

First, social workers indicated that workload pressures and service re-organisations afforded them less time to engage with other professionals. Jenny was critical of service changes in Almsbury. She told me that in cases where a social worker was needed to go out of the office to conduct a safeguarding enquiry, her team had to make requests to an adult community team. As there was often a delay before social workers were allocated, this caused a backlog for workers in the safeguarding teams, who were trying to manage current referrals. Jenny identified that this then affected her ability to engage with care home staff when conducting initial assessments of cases in their homes. She said:

'We have to request an allocation and wait for that to happen now. So, there's a lot of waiting for allocations and capacity. And because we have got such a volume to triage, I don't even pick up the phone to homes anymore. I haven't really got time to do that, because I have got to move on to the next one.' (From interview)

Jenny's case did not indicate that no one would speak to the homes in question. Rather, it showed that engagement with homes would be delayed until a social worker could be allocated to the case. This had the effect of weakening relationships between members of safeguarding teams and care homes. It also lessened opportunities for safeguarding issues to be resolved at an early stage.

Second, social workers in safeguarding teams were aware that where care agencies were experiencing financial crisis, they might not be able to engage with safeguarding processes. For example, social workers accepted that where agencies had severe staff shortages, as in the case of Complecare, their care staff would not be able to engage in safeguarding work because they would need to prioritise the urgent care needs which had been neglected by the service.

Shortages in funding also impacted on the social relations between social workers and service users. Nadia described a case in which gangs of sex workers in Fosborough were targeting "older vulnerable men". She reported that these men often wanted their relationships with the sex workers to continue because they were getting something from it, "whether it be a friendship, whether they think that's their girlfriend, whether they like the attention of someone young and attractive speaking to them" (from interview). Nadia felt that these men often had the mental capacity to make decisions about their finances, but identified that it would be useful to refer them to a place where they could meet with others, thus tackling their loneliness. She said:

'So, if say, for example, going back to somebody who may be socially isolated, hence why they are maintaining a friendship with a perpetrator, you know, so it might be that … the only available resources at that time is the day centre with, you know, which they attend, and it freaks them out because maybe they have not got dementia or they are in the early stages of dementia and everybody else there is much more advanced [but] that is frightening to them so that is more detrimental. Or at this time when I am looking for resources, there is no capacity out there in the community.' (From interview)

In Nadia's view, the lack of community resources available made it difficult for social workers to work flexibly around service users' needs. She also expressed frustration that social workers in adult community teams were encouraged to conduct safeguarding work as a short-term intervention. This made it hard to establish trust with service users so that they could discuss the type of abuse they were experiencing and what they might do to protect themselves. These limitations were also identified by other workers and viewed as short-termism, since the same service users would then be transferred back into the system following similar patterns of abuse. However, it is important to note that such pressures were viewed differently by different workers. For example, Margaret, a team manager, and other social workers in the same team gave examples of longer-term safeguarding work. It is difficult to judge the reason for this discrepancy, although it might have been that the team manager and other social workers were more experienced and so better practised in justifying their work in ways which would be deemed acceptable by their managers. Nonetheless, some social workers felt that a lack of resources would limit social relations in some cases. These limitations applied to work with other professionals and to work with service users.

Translating the safeguarding adults principles

While social workers believed that the lack of resources in social services made the application of policy difficult, they were still bound to work within it. In this section, I explain how social workers drew on the safeguarding principles laid out in law and guidance and how they were interpreted or shaped to allow for different types of work. From a risk work perspective, this process can be seen as one of knowledge translation (Gale et al, 2016), although this case involves policy being translated into interventions rather than research evidence. I show how these principles were used in diverse ways, with some practitioners using them to emphasise the need for person-centred practice and others using them to justify reducing services in line with resource constraints. As we saw in the Introduction and in Chapter 1, safeguarding decisions should be focused on the principles set out in the Care Act 2014, mainly the duty to promote wellbeing, under Section 1. Social workers should also work flexibly with individuals, applying the six principles of safeguarding set out in the *Care and Support Statutory Guidance* (DHSC, 2022, para 2.1): empowerment, prevention, proportionality, protection, partnership and accountability. I now look at how these principles were interpreted. I begin with interpretations of wellbeing, as this principle is intended by law to frame the others. I then set out the safeguarding adults principles, beginning with those which were talked about most often within interviews.

Wellbeing

Wellbeing is intended to be key to the Care Act 2014. Section 1 states that it is the general duty of a local authority when exercising functions under Part 1 of the Act 'to promote that individual's wellbeing' (Section 1(1)).[1] The principle is important because it highlights the centrality of service users' wishes and establishes that workers should begin with an assumption that an individual is best placed to judge what is in their own interests.[2] Prior to the Care Act 2014, eligibility for care and support was decided through the Fair Access to Care Services criteria (Department of Health, 2002), with local authorities deciding the level of need at which they would provide services (need was categorised as critical, substantial, moderate, or low). The eligibility criteria set out in The Care and Support (Eligibility Criteria) Regulations 2015 were intended to end what was in effect a postcode lottery.[3]

Notably, the principle of wellbeing was brought up rarely within interviews, with only three social workers mentioning it explicitly. Karen highlighted how safeguarding was linked to other duties. She said:

> 'if I have a safeguarding case, I will still apply the policy and legislation I would apply to other cases, you know. So, for example, if we assess under the Care Act eligibility for social care needs, we still use the care and we still look at the principle of prevention, of wellbeing. ... Yes, so it isn't, you know, that a safeguarding case is outside everything else. It is tied in like every other case.' (From interview)

In making this statement, Karen reflected current guidance, which states that practitioners should consider an individual's care and support and their wellbeing alongside any assessment of risk (LGA and ADASS, 2018).

Claire and Lisa used the term 'wellbeing' in a narrower way. Both participants drew on the term when assessing how well community or home care services were able to provide care to an individual. Claire said that she worried about the risk to one service user's wellbeing when she was being discharged from a hospital to her home. When asked to explain how she was using this term, she said:

'So, I was looking – there wasn't anything there to suggest that she wasn't – she didn't have any food or drink or that she – there were incontinence issues, but there was personal care being undertaken. There was no suggestion that she was having pressure sores or poor skincare. So it was, so what I'd seen about her, her general wellbeing. It didn't seem compromised that much.' (From interview)

Although Claire did not specifically refer to law and guidance, her account was concerned with the person's physical health. Lisa's account focused on a service user's control over the care he was provided. In this case, the term wellbeing was used to affirm his right to make a complaint about the care that he was receiving and to have the care agency who were providing his care acknowledge these concerns.

One social worker in the study, Patricia, questioned whether local authorities were able to implement the principles of the Care Act 2014 as intended:

Patricia: We simply haven't got the resources to do what used to be under [Fair Access to Care Services] [as] the moderate need.
Jeremy: Yes.
Patricia: So, the Care Act's very good on, 'it's all about wellbeing'. Well, that's bollocks. It's still critical.
Jeremy: Yes.
Patricia: You only get [a service] if [your need is] really high, substantial or critical, which doesn't exist anymore [under the Care Act]. But it's not true.

Patricia offered a blunt assessment of the impact of the Care Act 2014, arguing that due to limited resources local authority practice was operating a system of rationing, which should have been abolished under the Act.

Proportionality

Social workers highlighted ways in which local authorities attempted to rework principles of the Care Act 2014 and relevant guidance so that they fit with the need to manage finite resources. The local approaches effectively reshaped social work knowledge. For example, social workers in the Fosborough safeguarding team told me in a team meeting that their work was informed by the following principles and approaches:

(a) proportionality;
(b) Making Safeguarding Personal; and

(c) the three-tier model based on starting with [a] support conversation. Tier 1 – how can we help you help yourself (advice and information). Tier 2 – focused time-limited support. Tier 3 – High[ly] personalised support. (From field notes)

The principle of proportionality, one of the six principles in the *Care and Support Statutory Guidance* (DHSC, 2022), was mentioned first, with the other five principles remaining absent from the local authority's list. The Making Safeguarding Personal approach was listed second, reflecting its emphasis in national and local government guidance (DHSC, 2022; LGA, 2022a, 2022b). By contrast, the third entry on the list – a three tier-model encompassing supportive conversations – does not draw from government or sector guidance, but was obtained from a social care consultancy company, Partners for Change. The model was designed to help social work departments deliver personalisation within the constraints of austerity (Kirin, 2016). As mentioned in the previous chapter, social workers were somewhat sceptical about these sort of interventions and so adapted them to make the questions more sensitive to service users' situations. Overall, the local authority's approach worked on the premise that individuals should be encouraged to use their own resources where possible, although some workers would override the guidance where they viewed it as unjust.

In line with the approach taken in Fosborough, proportionality arose as a dominant theme in the data gathered in the other two local authorities, being mentioned more than any of the other principles in the *Care and Support Statutory Guidance* (DHSC, 2022). As noted in Chapter 3, proportionality is defined in current guidance as '[t]he least intrusive response appropriate to the risk presented', with the accompanying statement, 'I am sure that the professionals will work in my interest ... and they will only get involved as much as needed' (DHSC, 2022, para 14.13). Allowing service users to draw on their own resources was seen as the least intrusive response. Referring individuals to voluntary sector care and support services, such as a domestic violence support group, was also seen as a way of minimising intrusion. Where a service user had care and support needs, social workers in safeguarding teams argued that safeguarding risks should be dealt with within existing community services rather than through safeguarding processes. For example:

Amanda: One of the things that we might suggest at that point, before we take it into safeguarding, depending on what they've already tried, is have you had a multi-agency meeting to look at who's involved and who can do what?

Jeremy: Yes.

Amanda: I don't think it's proportionate to take that into safeguarding ... for safeguarding to do it when that can be done as part of a community multi-agency team.

Here, Amanda used the term 'proportionate' to signal where involvement from her own team was not appropriate; this mechanism was used by other workers too. The underlying message was that cases should be dealt with by existing services where possible. This could be services provided by adults community teams or by health services. Such interventions were positioned as being more acceptable to service users and seen as less likely to become coercive – for example, compelling a service user to clear their property under public health measures.

Other definitions of proportionality were used to signal where a service might not be offered. These interpretations appeared to stretch the intended meaning of proportionality within national policy. Kerry used the term to justify relying on CQC reports to make a judgement on the adequacy of a care home's response to a safeguarding concern, rather than assessing the concerns herself. This is reflected in the following extract:

Kerry: I think it [the Care Act] gave us the gift about proportionate response.
Jeremy: Yes.
Kerry: And so we do try and work with providers around ... so if it's a provider that I'm assured in, I know that CQC have rated them ...
Jeremy: Hmm.
Kerry: ... you know, and they're at least adequate, I would say, then I'm more reassured. And I think my proportionate knowing ... weighing everything makes me think, oh, actually, you know ... because we try and work with our providers, because I just feel on this occasion that there are too many variables where I'm just not happy to sort of park it.
Jeremy: Yes.
Kerry: Whereas with other ones [care home referrals], I would have probably said, actually, a proportionate response [is to not act].

Kerry's account indicated that social workers in safeguarding teams faced time pressures when trying to conduct safeguarding assessments. The use of the word "gift" in relation to the principle of proportionality suggests that the principle is used to justify using a lighter touch when engaging with care homes or nursing homes. Kerry suggested that social workers' level of intervention could be based on information in CQC inspection reports. She acknowledged that the effect of this reading was that she would be more likely to "park" concerns where homes had good CQC ratings and to act more coercively with homes with poor ratings (which was the case in this example). This interpretation was exceptional but indicated how the principle of proportionality could be reframed to respond to resource issues.

The term 'proportionality' was also used by teams to judge how other agencies responded. The following excerpt describes Isobel's reaction to a referral by a care home reporting an injury to one of their residents and how this was dealt with:

'[The care home reported that] when assisting [a resident] with care, bruises to [the] buttocks [were] noticed. Referral notes (a) skin broken – skin bundle put on and manual handling in place, (b) will discuss with GP on routine visit next week, (c) daughters made aware, (d) views – person happy and settled. Isobel – feels Section 42 [enquiry is needed] as [the] service user was bruised. Copies home's action plan into her plan. Speaks to senior practitioner, who advises actions proposed by carers [is] proportionate. Advises them to ask for a body map to be completed and reviewed, for manual handling and risk assessment process to be completed and for verbal reassurance from home that they will take action or reduce future incidents.' (From field notes)

This use of the term 'proportionate' was common within Isobel's team, particularly in relation to care providers. A proportionate response was often seen as one in which care providers had made other agencies aware of a medical concern or risk. This might be achieved by using the NHS 111 telephone service or by referring to a health visitor or a GP. Essentially the term was used to signal whether agencies had responded in an *adequate* way. Where agencies were deemed to have failed in this task, it was seen as appropriate to conduct a safeguarding enquiry.

Partnership and prevention

While proportionality was one of the dominant themes within the data, it was seen by many as overlapping with the themes of partnership and prevention. Partnership is defined within the *Care and Support Statutory Guidance* as '[l]ocal solutions through services working with their communities. Communities have a part to play in preventing, detecting and reporting neglect and abuse' (DHSC, 2022, para 14.13). Prevention is explained through the statement: 'It is better to take action before harm occurs' (DHSC, 2022, para 14.13). Several accounts by social workers focused on the need to encourage providers to think about safeguarding concerns, with an emphasis on the actions which should be taken by the providers or professionals in the first instance. For example, Amanda said:

> 'so we might be involved earlier on. We might not take that in for a full-blown, what we call safeguarding. It may not be proportionate to do that. But it might be that we are involved to give support and advice and information. It might be that we say to people … say, we've got a district nurse phoning up saying I'm really worried about this woman … she's doing that and I'm not quite … fine, we would talk it through.' (From interview)

Amanda's account linked partnership working to the principle of proportionality. She went on to identify where a case might be taken into safeguarding, and this indicated that an enquiry should only occur once it had been established that protection could not effectively be offered by another professional. In cases where safeguarding teams judged that the criteria for a Section 42 enquiry had been met, strategy meetings were seen as the best way of managing risk, alongside working with the service user as much as possible and involving them. Here, the terms 'partnership' and 'prevention' were primarily used to identify instances where the local authority should not be involved.

The principle of prevention was conceptualised differently in cases where a safeguarding enquiry had been undertaken. For example, Candice conducted a safeguarding enquiry with a service user in supported accommodation who feared her money was being stolen. The enquiry established that there was no hard evidence for this concern and that there was a suspicion that service user might be experiencing memory problems. Candice gave the service user information about how she might arrange for a CCTV (closed-circuit television) camera to be fitted. She assessed her intervention by saying: "But I think what has gone well is that she did thank me for contacting her and for the information about cameras, so she appreciated that advice and information. And in terms of safeguarding, I think it was more of prevention than, you know, taking active protection measures" (from interview).

In Candice's account, this intervention was seen as preventative in that it would help the service user feel safe and might also detect future theft if it was occurring. Similarly, social workers identified ways they might encourage care providers to develop preventative policies in relation to current safeguarding concerns. For example, Jenny described a case in which she had conducted a safeguarding enquiry for a woman in a care home who had experienced several falls. In this case, the provider was encouraged to look at the results of their own internal investigation and the safeguarding enquiry, and propose solutions. These actions were seen to be preventative in that they would lead to the development of local policies which would lower the likelihood of similar events happening in the future.

Protection

Although all workers spoke about cases in which protection was warranted, few related this to the principle set out in the *Care and Support Statutory Guidance*, which defines protection as '[s]upport and representation for those in greatest need' (DHSC, 2022, para 14.13). Where this was mentioned, social workers reflected on the tensions between promoting autonomy and providing protection, and on the need to provide different levels of protection plans. It is difficult to identify why this principle was not spoken about much, but it may be that the link between safeguarding and protection was seen as so obvious that it didn't need to be mentioned.

Empowerment

Empowerment is defined in the guidance as '[p]eople being supported and encouraged to make their own decisions and informed consent' (DHSC, 2022, para 14.13). Notably, only one worker – Ingrid – used the term 'empowerment' in interviews. Ingrid was working with a woman who had refused professional interventions, and she spoke about how talking to service users about abuse and neglect could give them the tools to empower themselves later. Although 'empowerment' was not mentioned specifically by the other social workers, they did talk about the points at which they felt that it was appropriate to provide service users with support and the degree to which the service users had been involved in decisions. Examples of this are given in the next chapter.

Accountability

The principle of accountability was mentioned by several social workers. This is described in current guidance as '[a]ccountability and transparency in delivering safeguarding' (DHSC, 2022, para 14.13). When using this term, social workers referred to the weight of responsibility they felt when conducting safeguarding work. Hayley spoke of the feelings of worry that she experienced as a social worker and then compared these with her feelings as a senior practitioner. She said:

> 'And now, as a safeguarding coordinator, I feel quite like a ... I think I feel a bigger sense of, kind of, accountability and responsibility, because it's me who's saying this is how we're going to approach it. This is the risk level, you know, we're going to associate with this. This

is how we're going to protect this. And also, then, my responsibility to show that I've done that thinking and I've done that work to make my decisions, so that recording of things.' (From interview)

Hayley went on to say that the weight of her responsibilities led her to feel an "underlying anxiety" due to the uncertainty inherent in decision-making. These anxieties were common among all the social workers. This was illustrated in talk about how they would present their case should "anything ever go to court" (Simon – from interview) or if they ever found themselves "in the dock" (Adrian – from interview). Workers had developed strategies to deal with this. For example, Simon noted that he demonstrated accountability through partnership working and double-checking accounts with other workers, and in working with them to develop a clear rationale for decision-making. His account aligned with Hayley's in that accountability was seen as being evidenced primarily in written records. Having discussions with senior practitioners and managers was also seen as helpful in making fewer defensive decisions. This was illustrated by Louise, who explained that "having that line of accountability up through management" (from interview) was useful in that it reassured practitioners that they did not hold sole responsibility for the case. Adrian identified that support from senior practitioners and managers enabled him to be aware of the effects of his own feelings on decision-making. In addition, he argued that working in partnership with the service user might reduce social workers' liability should things go wrong:

Adrian:	So, I'm perfectly accustomed to making risky, accountable … often being … often respecting someone's right to self-determination means that you make a more risky decision.
Jeremy:	Yes.
Adrian:	Rather than taking people's liberty away, which is often the easiest thing to do.
Jeremy:	Yes.
Adrian:	And having joint accountability means that you can make decisions that are riskier. Superficially riskier.

In Adrian's account, taking risks was part of the safeguarding process and was important as a means of minimising restrictions on people's liberty. He used the phrase "superficially riskier" to mark the distance between how other professionals might view the risk and how he and the service user viewed it after collaborative work. In taking this line, Adrian described an approach similar to 'positive risk taking' (Titterton, 2004, 2011), through which professionals can enable individuals to take risks which improve their quality of life, rather than reducing risks but limiting their quality of life (Robertson and Collinson, 2011).

Conclusion

This chapter used the framework of risk work to examine how social workers understood the principles of safeguarding. As we saw in the previous chapter, risk work within adult safeguarding involves interpreting law and policy. When talking about adult safeguarding, social workers frequently referred to changes in practice over time. The risk knowledge contained in safeguarding law and policy was viewed positively on the basis that the profession had rejected paternalism and accepted empowerment. In taking this line, social workers' accounts differed from perspectives in the critical literature which have aligned risk and personalisation with notions of individualisation (Webb, 2006; Ferguson, 2012).

Risk work theorists note that practitioners may question the truth of risk knowledge in some circumstances (Brown and Gale, 2018a). While social workers were positive about the notions of personalised safeguarding contained within current policy and guidance, they also identified a gap between policy ideals and what they were able to apply in practice. Social workers in the study felt that funding shortages had impacted on their ability to provide effective safeguarding services. This questioning of risk knowledge focused on three things. First, funding cuts led to higher thresholds been applied to health and social care services. This meant that safeguarding teams had to intervene more often, because safeguarding services were obliged to step in where other care services were failing or in financial difficulties. Second, staff shortages in safeguarding teams and adult community teams made safeguarding interventions less effective, as teams struggled to carry out enquiries in good time. Third, staff shortages impacted on social workers' social relations with care providers, either because delays eroded good relationships or because care staff had less capacity to engage with them during periods of crisis. In addition, social workers felt that lack of resources affected their social relations with service users, as they had no suitable resources to offer them.

Although social workers questioned current risk practices by highlighting the disparities between policy ideals and practice, they were still required to undertake safeguarding work, despite these limitations. As I identified in the previous chapter, knowledge translation in safeguarding work involves applying law and policy to a case, with the categories of risk and Section 42 criteria being key sources of knowledge. However, knowledge translation can also be seen as a pragmatic process through which certain principles are reframed to enable work to continue within existing service limitations. As a result of the limitations they experienced, social workers frequently reframed principles contained in the *Care and Support Statutory Guidance* (DHSC, 2022) to justify intervening less often. The principle of proportionality was used most frequently and was used as a justification for refusing an enquiry. The guidance indicates that proportionality means agencies should use the least intrusive response, and in one local authority this was put into practice using tools purchased to help the authority deliver personalisation in the context of austerity. This approach can be seen as an example of responsibilisation, as the aim of the tools was to get service users to draw on their own resources to manage risk wherever possible, thus minimising the need for local authority input. Similarly, the principle of proportionality was used to justify a lack of involvement where other services were already providing input. Social workers also used this principle to justify limiting their enquiries where risk information was available from other sources. Framings of the partnership principle were used to define instances where the local authority should not be involved. By contrast, the principle of prevention was used to identify instances in which service users might be signposted to services to help them feel safe. Certain principles were rarely cited – most notably empowerment and protection. While the principle of accountability is used within guidance to indicate what service users might expect of services, social workers' accounts focused on their own concerns about blame should things go wrong. To manage these concerns, social workers developed several informal interventions, such as careful documentation of risks and decision-making in multidisciplinary forums in order to share responsibility.

Doing adult safeguarding
with service users and carers

Introduction

In the previous chapter, I explained how social workers understood adult safeguarding principles and how they applied these to their work. This highlighted tensions between the ways social workers drew on law and policy as a source of risk knowledge and the limitations imposed on their interventions by austerity. Reductions in health and social care spending were seen to lead to safeguarding services being the "last stop", and this was seen as having an impact on the volume and complexity of safeguarding work. These pressures impacted on social relations by limiting the contact service users were able to have with professionals. The safeguarding principles embedded within the Care Act 2014 were interpreted in a variety of ways, with many using them to justify reducing services in line with resource constraints. In this chapter, I focus on the act of working with service users, family carers and care providers (such as care workers) when doing risk work within adult safeguarding. Specifically, I focus on the use of risk assessment tools, practical problems with person-centred safeguarding work and how social workers engage with service users and carers when assessing safeguarding risks and making safeguarding decisions.

Recording risks and negotiating responsibility: the use of risk assessment tools

As we saw in Chapters 2, 3 and 4, risk work involves translating risks into different contexts (Gale et al, 2016). Risk assessments form a core part of this process and can be understood as an intervention within the theoretical framework of risk work (Brown and Gale, 2018b). When using risk assessments, workers need to understand the types of knowledge they can draw on and how these might apply to the service users they are working with. In cases where workers can draw on research data to calculate the risk of an event occurring, the translation of risk involves the application of abstract data (risk knowledge) to individual cases. Where research data is not available, professionals may draw on other knowledge, such as personal experience or intuition (Zinn, 2016). As we saw in Chapter 2, several writers contend that the logic of statistics has driven risk assessment practice within social work (Webb, 2006, 2009; Pollack, 2010; Kemshall, 2016;

Doody et al, 2017). Arguments have also been made that risk assessment practices encourage 'responsibilisation' (O'Malley, 2009). In other words, social workers may encourage individuals, through education or warnings, to take on responsibilities which once would have been held by the state, with the state stepping in only where service users are unable or unwilling to manage their own risks (O' Malley, 2009). However, there is little research setting out how risk assessment procedures frame practice within adult safeguarding work. Adult safeguarding policy offers local authorities a large degree of freedom to set their own procedures (Dixon and Robb, 2016), and research confirms that risk assessment practice varies among local authorities (Manthorpe et al, 2015). To consider how social workers assessed and managed risk when working with adult safeguarding cases, we first need to turn to their understandings of risk assessment processes.

Risk assessments were used as an intervention in all local authorities in the study, although discrepancies were reported. Some social workers in Fosborough said that their local authority did not use risk assessments, or that they were only used in specific circumstances, such as when working with a service user with a pressure sore. In those cases, social workers reported drawing on their professional judgement. In other instances, social workers reported drawing on risk tools. Social workers in Gainsborough and Almsbury stated that they relied on paperwork intended to map the likelihood of risk. Judith, a social worker in Gainsborough, said:

'The risk matrix is the one where … so you've got like one to five down a column and then one to five on the header of likelihood and severity so, "it's very unlikely to happen" to "it's very likely to happen" and "it'll cause no harm" to "you're going to die". So that's the kind of scoring.' (From interview)

Accounts by Judith and others highlighted that risk matrices were used to make decisions about the tolerability of risk. No social workers referred to drawing on statistical or research evidence when completing risk assessments; rather, the measures were seen to reflect the opinions of professionals. In addition, workers in Gainsborough reported a shift in practice that placed greater emphasis on the service users' views of the risks and their preferred outcomes within the risk assessment paperwork. In other words, there was little evidence from my research that actuarial thinking was 'recasting' the nature of social work, as claimed by Webb (2009). None of the social workers in my sample believed that statistical knowledge was driving their practice. Rather, risk assessments were seen to be influenced by the six principles of safeguarding (DHSC, 2022), explored in the previous chapter.

While there was little evidence of actuarial thinking, risk assessments did shape practice in other ways. Rachel summarised the tools used in

Fosborough: "Yes, we used a risk tool to write down who was involved and what they felt the risks were. This helps so all agencies can know what each other are thinking ... it is a living document. We also write a risk chronology setting out what happened when" (from field notes). This account emphasised two elements of practice which have come to be favoured within both adult and children's settings. First, multidisciplinary meetings are thought to improve decision-making by providing multiple perspectives on risk (Robinson et al, 2019). Second, writing a risk chronology is thought to minimise the likelihood that important elements of a case will be missed (Stanley and Manthorpe, 2001). There was an acceptance from social workers across local authorities that risk documentation should be completed as part of strategy meetings and that this should act as summary of decision-making.

Social workers' descriptions of risk assessment work revealed certain beliefs about responsibility. They supported the view that meetings with the service user and other professionals helped to identify which risks were present. They also emphasised the way in which strategy meetings were used to attribute responsibility for risk taking to named individuals. On the face of it, these dynamics appear in line with responsibilisation theories. However, these theories often underplay the ability of social workers to make nuanced decisions in practice (McNeill et al, 2009). In line with Hannah-Moffat's (2005) criminological theories, social workers in my study were able to fuse concepts of risk and need and to consider how these concepts could be used therapeutically. Frequently, the intent behind social workers' actions was to highlight where service users had the right to take positive risks in their own lives, and risk assessments could be used to deflect paternalistic views that certain categories of people (such as those with a learning disability) could not take risks. Having established this principle, risk assessments were used to show which individuals could monitor or support risk taking. This information was used to demonstrate to agencies that it was reasonable to expect them to manage the risk within their organisation, rather then it being viewed as a safeguarding concern. This dynamic was found in Ingrid's interview where she spoke of working with Helen, who was living in supported housing. She said:

'The aims [of the strategy meeting] were to pass that responsibility back, pass that responsibility back, because I didn't have any doubts that she had capacity. I felt that she had capacity. I felt that this was something that they [the supported housing workers], working with her, should be able to manage, but they needed a bit of guidance about that. ... So, I really wanted to kind of be – what's the word? – a conduit to that really, to support that happening, but then be able to attract my involvement and to try and cover those kind of eventualities on that risk assessment, so that in the future they would have this working document that they would continue to review and just as a space really to record those thoughts.' (From interview)

In this case, the responsibility of managing the risk was seen by Ingrid to rest with the service user (on the basis that she had the mental capacity to make decisions about the risk) and the housing workers, who were there to support her. The risk assessment was viewed as a tool through which support workers might manage the risk in the future and as a way would lower the possibility of the case being presented as a safeguarding concern later. Thus, the risk assessment process was used to describe the responsibilities of other care agencies. Descriptions of using risk assessments to pass on responsibility were also given by other social workers in the study, with Amanda describing this as a way social workers might say to other professionals, "over to you now" (from interview). I explore the theme of responsibility and risk with both service users and carers in greater detail in the following sections.

Person-led safeguarding: practical issues and problems

As we saw in previous chapters, social relations play a key part in risk work. As Brown and Gale (2018b) note, intervening on the basis of risk knowledge is always a moral act, and it has the potential to affect relationships between social workers, service users, carers or other professionals. Legislation and policy in England indicates that adults should have a central place in decision-making about their care, including safeguarding (DHSC, 2022). However, previous research has shown that these policies are not always applied as intended (McDonald, 2010). Social workers have been seen to have mixed views as to whether service users are offered real choices or only theoretical ones during safeguarding (such as only being given choices where the local authority agrees with the service user; Stevens et al, 2018). Studies have also found that people with care and support needs are often unaware of the formal safeguarding processes their cases undergo at local authority level (Aspinal et al, 2019). To explore these issues in greater depth, this section examines social worker perspectives on service user involvement in safeguarding, including what circumstances they would seek to involve them and where they might avoid doing so.

Social workers in my study believed that the social work profession championed service user choice and control. As described in Chapter 4, it was common for social workers to make favourable comparisons between their own practice and that of health professionals, who were often painted as being risk-averse or overprotective. However, when speaking about their own practice, social workers tended to make more qualified statements about service user involvement. Several reasons were given for not informing service users about a safeguarding referral or not involving them in a decision. I present each of these next.

Are they safe now? Establishing the person's immediate safety

Social workers across local authorities supported the principle of service user involvement, but highlighted the need to establish whether the person who had been referred was safe. Nicola gave examples in her interview, including a referral which had come in reporting that a care agency had missed several visits to a service user. Nicola said:

'my first instinct would have been to check that actually they were both safe and they had both had ... sort of look at the immediate situation, how to rectify that immediately ... to make sure that they had had food, water, somebody to support them to get to the toilet, have their personal care, etc., etc.' (From interview)

Here, Nicola focused on the need to meet service users' immediate physical care needs. This need to act to ensure service users' immediate safety, where the safeguarding criteria were met, was also applied by social workers in referrals relating to care homes. Social workers indicated that such actions did not preclude the person being involved in safeguarding assessments, but this part of the assessment should be delayed until the person's immediate physical safety was assured.

"It wasn't very practical to speak to him on the phone": the need for face-to-face assessments

Judgements about risks and how they should be handled are invariably sensitive. Previous research has indicated that maintaining trust and communicating risks diplomatically are important elements of risk work (Brown and Calnan, 2012; Gale et al, 2017). These dynamics were highlighted by social workers when discussing who should speak to a service user or carer about a safeguarding concern. A common issue raised by social workers conducting assessments from the office was concern about the suitability of telephone assessments. In raising this issue, social workers were not saying that the person who had been referred for a safeguarding assessment should not be spoken to; rather, they were making the argument that they should not be the one to do it. For example, Rebecca said:

'in this case, it wasn't very practical to speak to him over the phone, because he seems to have some learning difficulties. There is some really complicated family dynamics. So, I think the phone call wouldn't make any sense to them – like, who I'm calling, why I'm calling. You know? And to explain it. And I would probably cause more damage than, you know, bring any benefits to this. We always tend to speak to people when there is, for example, financial abuse or any allegations or anything, you know, when you know the phone call will bring more clarity. ... But in this case, it wouldn't be beneficial, really, at this stage.' (From interview)

Rebecca gave this service user's potential learning difficulties as the reason for requesting an in-person assessment. This justification was also used by other social workers for service users living with dementia. These cases were viewed to be problematic because service users with these needs might lack capacity to make decisions relating to abuse or neglect. An in-person assessment was deemed necessary because it would allow for a better quality of mental capacity assessment. Complex family dynamics, as mentioned by Rebecca, were given by several social workers as a reason for having an in-person assessment. This was due to the social workers' awareness that perpetrators might intimidate victims and that it would be difficult to observe or manage this unless you could see what was happening in the room. The need to address sensitive issues was also seen as a reason for face-to-face assessment. For example, Mike spoke of a case in which a neighbour raised a suspicion that a carer may be having a sexual relationship with a service user; he explained, "I didn't want to have that conversation with an 80-year-old woman on the phone" (from interview). While these arguments were logical, they also needed to be weighed against resource issues, with workers in Fosborough being aware that a face-to-face enquiry by an adult community team may not occur for several months.

"I wouldn't know her if she walked past me in the street": working with resistance

Making Safeguarding Personal policies highlight the importance of discussing risk with individuals and establish the principle that safeguarding should be done with, not to, people. Policy portrays service users as 'rational actors' who will want to weigh up the costs and benefits of risk taking in their own lives (Kemshall, 2010). In this scenario, social relations between adult social workers and service users are positioned as unproblematic. In line with previous research, social workers in my study were positive about the aims of the Making Safeguarding Personal initiative (Butler and Manthorpe, 2016; Cooper et al, 2016; Cooper et al, 2018). However, they highlighted difficulties in engaging with service users. This issue was raised by Margaret when speaking about a service user in one of her safeguarding cases. She said:

'It is not about taking over, is it? And it's about working, you know, to find what's important for her. The trouble with people like her is you know they don't engage so how do you actually find out, you know? ... I've never met her, I wouldn't know her if she walked past me in the street.' (From interview)

The issue was also illustrated in my interview with Adrian, who spoke of going to visit a service user for whom he had received a safeguarding referral:

Adrian: Yes. I went with the intensive housing services worker to try and see him and he ... we knocked for ages and then we assumed he wasn't there. And then I knocked on the window and he came in and he closed the curtains and he ...
Jeremy: Right.
Adrian: ... opened the door, looked out, and he closed it again. So, it was quite a clear sense that he didn't want to ...
Jeremy: Did he know who you were? Or ...
Adrian: I ... Just trying to balance the shouting outside someone's front door that you're a social worker, which isn't a very nice thing to do to someone, is it? But with also kind of trying to explain, in a way, that he ... I kind of said through his letterbox in a reasonably loud voice that I was a social worker and I wanted to have a quick chat with him because people were concerned.
Jeremy: Yes. So did he respond at all when you chatted through the letterbox? Or ...
Adrian: No, no, no. Didn't say anything.
Jeremy: No?
Adrian: He just saw us and closed the door in an assertive, slammy sort of way that suggested I'm not going to speak to you or you're not coming in.

Adrian's interview describes a common practical difficulty experienced by social workers – that safeguarding concerns are often raised by professionals rather than with the service users themselves. In these cases, service users might have little or no interest in engaging in a conversation about managing perceived risks. While Adrian realised that communication through the letterbox was problematic, he spoke later in the interview about his lack of powers to force engagement.

While social workers felt that their end aim was to try and engage the service user in the safeguarding process, they were also aware that they had few statutory powers through which to do so. To promote engagement, social workers worked with other professionals to consider what steps might be taken to build trust. This might be achieved through encouraging GPs or nurses to offer health appointments to raise concerns (in cases where these workers were viewed by the service user as less threatening than social services). In addition, social workers would look for opportunities where service users might have an incentive to meet with them, such as when they were looking for housing or benefits, or were keen to escape an abusive partner (this issue is explored in more detail later in the chapter).

Difficulties of engaging with service users within the time available

As mentioned earlier, in my interviews with social workers, they offered several justifications for not engaging with service users. However, there were some instances where social workers failed to talk with service users, and they left this unremarked or struggled to offer a justification. For example, Lisa worked on a case where an older man had told his nurse that home carers had been too rough with him when helping him to change into his clothes or pyjamas and that this had resulted in a cut to his skin. The nurse had then made a safeguarding referral. During the morning, Lisa made telephone calls to the care agency and to the service user's wife to get their account of the incident. I asked Lisa why she had not spoken to the service user:

Lisa: I would ideally [have] liked to have spoken to Mr ...
Jeremy: OK, yes. So what stopped you speaking to him do you think, in that case?
Lisa: Because her [the service user's wife] account was so clear, you know, and yes, her account was so clear.
Jeremy: Yes, OK. So, her account was clear. So just to confirm further ...
Lisa: She was a witness. She saw it.
Jeremy: OK. So just to be devil's advocate. Why do you think you wouldn't ask him as well, in that case?
Lisa: Yes, I don't know. I don't know. Because ... I don't know.
Jeremy: Yes.
Lisa: Yes, I could go back. And, yes, I don't know why I didn't ask to speak to him. Yes, how much evidence can I gather? But, yes, true, I could have spoken to him.

Lisa was honest enough to acknowledge that she did not know why she had not contacted the service user in question. Her comment "how much evidence can I gather?" suggests that she had to decide how to allocate a finite amount of time. Her remark that the service user's wife was "such a good witness" also suggests that she may have viewed her account as being as reliable as his. Similarly, other social workers struggled to articulate why they had not spoken directly to the individuals concerned. While it is difficult to be certain about why service users were not spoken to in these situations, it was clear that social workers in safeguarding teams were under considerable pressure to clear, or at least keep on top of, referrals into the system, as outlined in Chapter 3. In other words, the issue of time appeared to be a key factor and has parallels with findings from the child protection literature in which social workers had to balance the time it took to input information to ICT systems against the time that could be spent with service users (Shaw et al, 2009). These service pressures may explain the gap between best practice, as outlined by practitioners, and having information viewed as 'good enough' for the purposes of initial assessment.

Working with service users during safeguarding enquiries

As we saw in the previous section, social workers positioned their profession as championing good safeguarding practice, but also provided justifications about where this was not possible. These accounts focused on some of the tensions with conducting risk work, namely the problem of overcoming service user suspicions and resistance, the problems inherent in assessing risk from a distance and the limits to engagement caused by time restrictions. While building and establishing social relations are a core part of risk work, they also give rise to complex dynamics. These include the ways in which risk is explained and the extent to which such explanations build trust or alienate service users (Brown and Calnan, 2012; Gale et al, 2017). Next, I focus on the actions social workers took to try to build trust with service users during safeguarding assessments. I begin by considering how social workers explained what safeguarding was.

Explaining adult safeguarding

To engage with individuals around risk, professionals need to be clear about the frameworks through which it is defined as well as their own role in addressing it. Such interactions rely on relational transparency – often viewed as a key value among social workers, though what this means in practice is often ambiguous (Dons et al, 2022). Social workers in my study emphasised the value of being transparent with service users about what safeguarding was. For example:

Adrian: I think I've learned to be blunter and in general that's better. Although it's not always better, but it quite often is.
Jeremy: Yes. And why do you think it's better to be blunter in most situations?

Adrian:	I think most people value candour, and it's also fairer looking at values.
Jeremy:	Yes, yes.
Adrian:	And I wouldn't like the idea of someone doing something to me under law without me knowing.
Jeremy:	Yes. So it's about being explicit, really, about what's happening?
Adrian:	Yes.
Jeremy:	Yes. OK.
Adrian:	Because if not, you are in danger of it being about your fear as a practitioner, aren't you?
Jeremy:	Yes
Adrian:	And how you're going to deliver this information and how it's going to make you look and make you feel.

In this extract, Adrian indicated that transparency is important because service users had the right to know when a legal process was taking place. He described the process of explaining safeguarding as being "blunter" with service users, indicating that it was important to explain things in a way which could be easily understood. Adrian qualified his statement by saying that "it's not always better, but it quite often is". Nonetheless, his account focused on the importance of explaining his professional role where possible. Adrian's account also acknowledged the emotional impact of holding the safeguarding role. This demonstrated an awareness of how social workers might be perceived as well as societal expectations about how such risks should be managed; an issue that child protection workers have also been found to be sensitive to (Warner, 2015).

Most social workers in my study highlighted that service users were normally unaware as to what adult safeguarding was. Because of this, they had to construct explanations to explain their role. Nicola provided one example of this when describing how she talked to service users:

Nicola:	First of all, do they understand what ... so I always start by saying this is who I am.
Jeremy:	Yes.
Nicola:	This is what safeguarding is and I say safeguarding, but I kind of always try and say, I think, what does safeguarding mean. So, I always sort of say the council's got responsibility to make sure people are free from abuse.
Jeremy:	Yes.
Nicola:	And we want to keep you safe. I try and paraphrase it like that.
Jeremy:	Yes.
Nicola:	Because otherwise it's a bit of a meaningless [laughs].

Here, Nicola gave a simplified version of the Section 42 criteria, highlighting the local authority's duty to make enquiries into abuse or neglect, though she omitted to mention that this duty only applied to those with care and support needs. Penny also spoke of the need to explain what adult safeguarding was, but she used an alternative strategy. She described likening adult safeguarding to the child safeguarding process:

'I think people do understand child protection a lot, child safeguarding, I guess, in a lot more ... than they do adults. It's still not an area that ... and I guess people do find it really, really difficult to understand why you'd be worried about certain things, because in their minds they wouldn't be worried about it.' (From interview)

While child safeguarding is quite different from adult safeguarding, this analogy is used to show the difference between risks the person is subject to and the risks caused by their own behaviours. Penny's account also highlighted the difficulties of working with service users on safeguarding where their interpretation of risk was different to that of the person who had raised the concern. Nonetheless, such explanations were seen as important to opening conversations and establishing whether the person understood the safeguarding concern.

"People are allowed to take risks": promoting the principles of the Mental Capacity Act 2005

In previous chapters, I explained that a central part of risk work for social workers is interpreting law and policy. Specifically, I showed how safeguarding practice drew on the Care Act 2014 and the *Care and Support Statutory Guidance* (DHSC, 2022). Previous research with safeguarding adults coordinators reported that they were hopeful that the Mental Capacity Act 2005 would gain momentum (Manthorpe et al, 2013). Social workers in my research highlighted that often professionals were ignorant of the Mental Capacity Act 2005 or misunderstood how it should be applied, a point that has also been made by a government review (House of Lords, 2014). Risk work thus entailed ensuring that the principles of the Act were promoted. For example, Marcia gave an account of housing professionals asking for a service user's wishes to be overruled because she had a learning disability, was using drugs and was being financially exploited. She said: "I came into working with Helen in the assumption that she did have capacity, and nothing that she said or did during our conversations made me doubt it" (From interview). In this account, Marcia highlighted that her work had been informed by the first principle of the Mental Capacity Act 2005 – that is "a person must be assumed to have capacity unless it is established that he lacks capacity" (Section 1(2)). This principle was then judged as the foundation on which future collaborative work might be based.

Social workers also indicated that the principles of the Mental Capacity Act 2005 were important because they enabled service users to take capacitated decisions about risk. For example, Sue said:

'I mean some agencies can be quite, you know, there is a risk there, and we have got a, you know, smother this person in cotton wool ... and then you need to sort of remind people that there is such a thing as sometimes positive risk taking, or there is such a thing as people being surrounded by risk but having the capacity to make their own decision to say well this is my decision. This is what I want to happen.' (From interview)

To highlight social workers' role in promoting positive risk taking, Sue provides an exaggerated account of defensive practice in which professionals wish to "smother" the person in "cotton wool". Social workers also regularly referred to the principle under the Mental Capacity Act 2005 that 'a person is not to be deemed as unable to make a decision merely because he makes an unwise decision' (Section 1(4)). For example, Claire said, "I mean we [social services] recognise that people are allowed to take risks and are allowed to make unwise decisions, but I don't think other organisations always do" (From interview). While allowing service users to make 'unwise decisions' was seen to be core to the Mental Capacity Act 2005, several social workers spoke of their discomfort in doing so. For example, Mavis said: "We feel very powerlessness around self-neglect ... [There is] nothing you can do. The person's making an unwise decision" (From interview).

While allowing service users to make unwise decisions was seen to be important for their autonomy, social workers also felt that this trapped them in a difficult cycle. This occurred for two reasons. First, social workers indicated that they were under pressure to close cases where a person was identified as making unwise decisions, meaning that their role in preventing further abuse was likely to be limited. Second, social workers argued that some service users who made unwise decisions might experience further abuse and neglect. For example, Patricia indicated that the service user she was working with would be likely to go "downhill" once she had closed the case, and this was likely to lead to a further safeguarding referral in the future.

While social workers referred regularly to the principles of the Mental Capacity Act 2005, it was surprisingly rare for them to talk about the concept of 'best interests' in relation to their own interactions with service users. This issue only arose where individuals with lasting powers of attorney were judged not to be discharging their duties properly, or during work on cases with Court of Protection involvement. Similarly, the possibility of using a Mental Capacity Act advocate was only touched on in passing by a few social workers.

"It's about working ... to find what's important to her": assessing service user views of risk

As stated in Chapter 2, risk assessment tools have often been built on the assumption that service users will assess and manage risk in rational ways (Kemshall, 2010). Research in the 1990s and 2000s led to a questioning of this assumption, showing that individuals judged by professionals to be taking irrational risks are often acting in ways that are rational to them (Kemshall, 2014). Social workers in my study highlighted the need to see the risk from the service user's perspective. This process required a degree of empathy. Margaret said: "yes, it is, you know, put yourself in her shoes and think, oh my goodness me, I wouldn't want that life. But it is about as well, isn't it, it's about how she sees the risks and how she managed the risks herself you know" (From interview). Margaret's reference to putting herself in her service user's shoes alongside her statement that "I wouldn't want that life" were used to signal the difference between her own values and those which might be held by service users. These points were commonly used by other social workers in the study to describe situations they would wish to avoid – most commonly situations where the individual was living with an abuser or where a person was living in housing that other professionals viewed as insanitary.

Social workers' awareness that service users' view of risk might differ from their own informed the assessment process. This was illustrated by Rachel, who said:

'Well, in one of our other cases, there was an Asian woman who was working as a street worker. This was reported to us by another agency. They were concerned by a number of risks, such as the woman continuing to work as a street worker and taking drugs. However, we asked the woman what she thought about the risks. For her, the main risk was being abducted by her family. She had taken quite careful measures not to go within 25 miles of where her family were living. So, in her mind, she was taking steps to reduce the risks that were important to her. So this is important, because it can show professionals that people are talking about risk, although it may not be the type of risks that professionals are talking about. And the person is making an informed decision.'

Rachel's account worked to give context to the service user's decision-making and to show how risk taking which appeared unwise or irrational to professionals (engaging in sex work) was rational to the service user because it lowered the risks that mattered to her (abduction by her family). From this perspective, it was seen as important to engage with those risks which mattered to the service user before seeking to manage them.

Social workers recognised that some service users routinely lived in risky situations and therefore had a high level of tolerance for risk taking. This level of tolerance would be considered when social workers were conducting risk assessments. For example:

Nicola: [What] I will always ask is, 'are you scared?' ... I was working with a woman who was a drug user, she was pregnant, so Children's Services were involved for that side. She was in an abusive relationship, but that was oddly how she functioned, so in what would seem like a very risky situation to you or I. She would minimise the risk.

Jeremy: Yes.

Nicola: But actually [she] might feel oddly safe in that situation because it was her normal. Does that make sense?

Jeremy: Yes.

Nicola: So, that's why I always try. If someone like that then said they were frightened, then I would be actually quite worried. Do you see what I mean? So, you have got to make your risk assessment on the context of their situation as well.

Nicola's account highlighted the high degree of risk that the service user normally lived with. The phrase "that was oddly how she functioned" was used to indicate that the service user had become acclimatised to a high degree of risk taking. However, this high tolerance for risk taking was seen as an important consideration when assessing the service user's perspectives on her risk. Where the service user expressed fear, this was immediately judged to be serious, because she had a high threshold for danger.

"You don't have to take it": working with service users to promote safety

Gale et al argue that 'caring in the context of risk produces a fundamental challenge in risk work between negotiating "normality" and "risk"' (2016, p 1064). As we have seen, social workers saw a need to respect service users' choices to take unwise decisions, and they were also aware that what might be deemed as risky choices within the general population were often 'normal' choices for their service users. Nonetheless, social workers were concerned to build relationships with service users to help them to consider the abuse and neglect they were experiencing and to help them take actions to prevent such abuse in the future. Social workers in both safeguarding teams and adult community teams sought to give these messages to service users. Social workers in the safeguarding team in Fosborough only worked with service users by telephone, and so faced greater challenges in their ability to build relationships with service users. Social workers in this team did make efforts to make it clear to individuals that they did not have to tolerate abuse. For example, I heard Claire emphatically telling a woman who was experiencing domestic abuse about the services on offer. This was underlined by the statement, "You don't have to take it, Michelle" (from field notes).

Social workers based in safeguarding teams in Gainsborough and Almsbury and those in adult community teams had greater opportunities to assess and work with service users face to face. For example, Nadia told me about her work with a victim of domestic violence. She said:

Nadia: So, one of the things that came up today was she said to me through lots and lots of questions, you just don't get to this point. She said to me that her boyfriend had blackouts and attacks her, and he attributed those blackouts to cannabis. His cannabis use.

Jeremy: Right.

Nadia: So, I wanted to explore with her … does that make it OK, because he's having a blackout and he doesn't know what he is doing? Does that mean he can still harm you? So it's do you think that's right? You know, that sort of thing, so you are exploring it a little bit more to their understanding and whether they feel that it is acceptable or it is not acceptable.

Jeremy: Yes, yes.

Nadia: And in this particular case, she actually said to me I don't believe him when he says that he has blackouts. I think he knows what he is doing.

Jeremy: Right.

Nadia: But I would have never have got that statement from her had I not of explored a little bit more detail in terms of is that right that he hits you just because he's having a blackout.

In this extract, Nadia discussed the importance of building relationships with service users experiencing abuse and encouraging them to think about aspects of the abuser's behaviour. The process which Nadia described is similar to the process of 'chipping away', which Robb (2021) describes in her interviews with social workers who work with women with learning disabilities experiencing domestic violence. Within this process, social workers focused on helping service users by encouraging incremental changes. In Nadia's example, the service user chose to stay with the abuser, but the work was seen as valuable in fostering the service user's insight into her situation. These types of intervention were described by other social workers in relation to financial abuse cases. For example, Ingrid reflected on a strategy meeting with a service user called Helen, who was engaged in sex work, was using drugs and was experiencing financial abuse from others. Ingrid said:

> 'But I would hope at the least that that process of allowing Helen that space to talk confidently and honestly about her needs and have that insight within that space was cathartic and provided her with maybe some empowerment to protect herself better in the future and maybe some empowerment when she's in a situation where somebody asks her for money or asks her to come out and she's just been paid. To have that moment of insight – do you know what, I'm worth more than that, I'm not going to do that today.' (From interview)

As noted previously, Ingrid was the only social worker to refer explicitly to the principle of empowerment in her research interview. However, her description of allowing Helen to discuss her situation was in line with other accounts, and the aim here was to enable the person to protect themselves better in the future. The interventions focused on helping the person establish self-esteem and act more assertively in the future. These practices also involved directing service users to available sources of support so that they could access support in the future if needed.

Engaging with family carers and paid carers around abuse and neglect

In this section, I focus on risk work with family carers and paid carers, such as care workers, around abuse and neglect. The character of these interactions was different to those with service users: social workers' interactions with service users were concerned with respecting their autonomy, whereas their interactions with carers were about dealing with individuals who had been accused of being abusive or neglectful. Because of this, social workers faced the dilemma of whether to exercise care, by providing support to families, or control, by assertively implementing laws and policies. Previous research has shown that social workers are somewhat ambivalent about the use of legal powers within adult safeguarding (Stevens et al, 2020). In England, powers of entry were consulted on but not enacted, but the research demonstrates there is a range of attitudes among social workers to exercising care and control within this area. When asked whether they favoured being given new powers of entry to safeguard adults, most were in favour, though many argued that such powers would negatively affect relationships with service users and their families and would be in conflict with social work values. Consequently, it is important to consider how legal responsibilities are managed alongside relationships and whether law and policy are strictly applied, as professionals may use law and policies flexibly when managing risks (Horlick-Jones, 2005). I begin this discussion by focusing on how social workers interacted with family carers.

Working with family carers

As mentioned earlier, intervening on the basis of risk knowledge is always a moral act, and it has the potential to affect relationships between social workers, service users, carers or other professionals (Brown and Gale, 2018b). Risk work involves decisions about how to present information about risk to service users and carers. As risk is often associated with blame, both by professionals and the public (Douglas, 1992), relationships of openness and trust can be difficult to maintain within statutory practice (Hyslop and Keddell, 2018). Consequently, the nature of the relationship between the social worker and the person they are working with is likely to be key in the operation of risk work (Murphy et al, 2013).

Two approaches to working with family carers were evidenced in the data. First, some social workers framed their interactions with carers as a supportive intervention. In doing so, they highlighted the value which family carers brought to society. For example, when talking about a case where a relative had been accused of abusing a family member with support needs, Lisa began by highlighting the potential needs of the carer:

Lisa: Carers are, you know, a goldmine for this organisation. We [are] stretched and need to take care of the carers, you know?

Jeremy: Yes.

Lisa: Carers come on my top list, you know? They are people … absolutely we couldn't function, you know? Talking of our resources and organisation, we could not, you know, we could not function if it wasn't for so many carers out there providing care for their loved ones or their neighbours or for a relative, you know?

Jeremy: Yes.

Lisa: So, to me, [with] my organisational hat, [I] would say look after that carer, you know?

Jeremy: Right.

Lisa: Send somebody out, offer an assessment. It might be that we might retrieve … be able to help the situation. If we can't, you know, I mean it could be that it is irretrievable, but at the first stage, you know, let's look after the carers who look after vulnerable adults. (From interview)

Lisa argued that the local authority should value family carers because they provide care for little financial reward, and this was of value to the local authority. Lisa's statement that "carers come on my top list" and her reference to carers looking after "loved ones" indicated her view that the starting position towards family carers should be supportive. Her reference to an assessment also indicated that support might be provided via a carers assessment under the Care Act 2014. While she did not rule out that an enquiry might lead to the decision that the situation was "irretrievable", she positioned carers as morally good until proved otherwise, and emphasised the need to engage in an empathic way.

Lisa's line of reasoning was common, with social workers starting from a position that abuse or neglect might be present due to carer stress. This affected how explicit carers were willing to be about the safeguarding concerns raised. Several workers indicated that they downplayed the safeguarding concern when seeking to engage with carers. This manifested itself in two ways. Louise was working with an older woman who was living at home with her husband and had been reported to be losing weight. Nurses in the area had made a safeguarding referral, expressing concern that the husband was not feeding his wife appropriately. Louise said:

'I mean, I'm not sure that it would help or serve a purpose to use the term "safeguarding adults". Yes, I don't think it would have been necessary to, and I think that he [the husband and carer] probably would have been really upset. They might have both been really upset by the idea that anyone could think that he'd be abusing or neglecting her, even if it was unintentional ... I wouldn't want him to feel suspicious of Social Services or feel reluctant to tell people things and work alongside us. You know. And you know, I did want to be supportive to him as well as her.' (From interview)

In making the argument that she should not be explicit with the carer about the safeguarding process, Louise displayed an empathic response to him, highlighting the negative impact on the relationship which might occur between the social worker and the family should he feel that he was being blamed. Louise did not rule out telling the carer that a safeguarding concern had been raised at a later point, but stated that she would only do so if there was a "really good reason, a really good benefit". In other words, she sought to weigh up the risk of being explicit about the safeguarding concern against the risk to the relationship with the family, with a blunt response being viewed as inappropriate unless evidence emerged that the carer was abusing his wife.

Simon demonstrated another supportive approach, downplaying safeguarding in a different way. He spoke of assessing a case where a man with a learning disability who lived with his father and brother had been referred to safeguarding due to concerns about self-neglect and hoarding. There had also been some concerns that the father may have been financially exploiting the service user. Within the interview, the social worker drew parallels between his own biography and that of the father. This account sought to build empathy by highlighting the financial and cultural difficulties which both he and the father had lived through in Fosborough in the 1970s, alongside a hope that the father had "matured and mellowed". He said:

'So, some of that was sort of informal education to the father really. You know. Just to say, you know, you have to be careful because, you know, if there is a concern about how you're managing your son's finances, then there will be an investigation into it. Whether that's police, whether it's local authority, and it might get flagged up to the police.' (From interview)

Simon's account of the similarities between the father and himself were used to frame the safeguarding intervention as "informal education" rather than an as an official process under the Care Act 2014 or other legislation. Notably, Simon disassociated himself from local authority processes by warning that further concerns might lead to an investigation by the local authority or the police (despite being employed by the local authority himself).

A second approach towards family carers was to be assertive about the problems. This was used less commonly. Here, social workers emphasised the need to be explicit with family members about the nature of the safeguarding concern from an early stage. Marcia, a manager in Fosborough, recounted a case where a son who had lasting power of attorney for his mother's finances was alleged to be spending her money on himself and neglecting to pay her bills. After delegating the case to a social worker in her team to make enquiries, Marcia had called a strategy meeting to make her concerns explicit to the son. She said:

'I felt the easiest thing to do with these cases is just to be transparent and say, look, this is the situation, this is what's being alleged ... I wanted to see him and how he responded and see him face to face, because I think that's quite important with safeguarding. I really think that it's about engaging the person at the centre but other family members also.' (From interview)

In contrast to the previous social workers, Marcia described engagement as a process of assessing the responses of the family member. This was seen as a means of assessing whether they were telling the truth, alongside cross-checking their accounts with other parties – in this case, the local authority finance department. In her interview, Marcia spoke of the need to educate the carer about his lasting power of attorney responsibilities. Warnings were also issued in the meeting about Marcia's power to refer the case to the Court of Protection should further financial concerns come to light. In other words, the meeting was used to set out legal and moral expectations around the carer's management of his mother's finances, with assertive monitoring being used to ensure that further abuse did not occur.

Working with care providers

In the previous section, I identified how social workers highlighted the need to maintain openness and trust when doing risk work with family carers. Concerns about carers being alienated through feelings of blame led to most social workers emphasising their role in facilitating support, although some indicated the need to challenge family members about alleged abuse. Different dynamics came into play when social workers were working with care providers – a term I use here to refer to care workers or managers in care homes or nursing homes. Risk work is influenced by dynamics of power and accountability within organisational settings (Brown and Gale, 2018a). These dynamics are relevant in adult safeguarding work and act to frame knowledge, interventions and social relations. As we saw in Chapter 1, the abuse and neglect of older adults in institutional settings is a longstanding issue, with campaigners highlighting incidences in public services since the 1960s. Government laws and policies in relation to elder abuse in care homes aim to protect the vulnerable, while also maintaining the goal of reducing the size of the state (Manthorpe and Stevens, 2015). This has led to policies focused on regulating the social care workforce (Burns et al, 2013). This then frames social relations. As key decision-makers within safeguarding enquiries, social workers hold authority over those within the social care workforce who are subject to such regulations. Next, I show that social workers' views of safeguarding with care providers focused on assessing and monitoring the regulation of their work.

"Holding themselves accountable": expectations on reporting by care providers

As mentioned earlier, risk work in social work involves interpreting law and policy, and the Care Act 2014 and its guidance and the Mental Capacity Act 2005 were commonly used to inform practice. However, other laws and policies are also relevant when working with care agencies. Under the Health and Social Care Act 2008, care providers have a statutory 'duty of candour'. This requires providers who are regulated under the CQC to be open and transparent with service users, their families and advocates where a 'notifiable safety incident' occurs (see Note 4 in Chapter 1). Regulations also state that providers must report specific harms to the CQC, including abuse or allegations of abuse (The Care Quality Commission (Registration) Regulations 2009). However, a dominant expectation among social workers in the study was that care providers should report any incidents which might be construed as abuse or neglect to the local authority under Section 42 of the Care Act 2014. While not supported in current law and policy, this expectation was viewed as care providers' responsibility. Self-reporting any potential incidences of abuse and neglect was consequently positioned as a moral duty. For example, Mike, said:

'we want to hear if there is a concern and that it is not necessarily an admission of fault or that somebody is to blame for what has happened, but it may just be that there has been an accident or something has happened that we need to be made aware of.' (From interview)

This view was reflected by Isobel She said: "I think for them to see themselves as accountable that this happened, and it shouldn't have happened – we need to report this. ... Holding themselves accountable for that ... the behaviour shows me that service users are being looked after" (From interview). Isobel's comment reflected a dominant belief among social workers. Care homes who self-reported concerns were portrayed as good citizens by social workers, and those who failed to do so were viewed with suspicion. Expectations around self-reporting had been internalised by care providers, who regularly self-reported such issues or concerns. These referrals included errors by care staff which may have led to harm, such as missed visits to a service user, forgetting to give a service user their prescribed medication or resident-on-resident abuse. They also included harms to service users which did not necessarily indicate abuse or negligence but could be construed in this way. These cases included older service users receiving cuts or scratches and residents in care homes being injured from falls, becoming dehydrated or developing pressure sores. Most social workers believed that encouraging care providers to self-report enabled local authorities to identify recurrent concerns over time. In other words, an single case might not be seen as a concern, but several incidences could indicate problems with a care provider.

"I expect them to be saying things that I would find reassuring": trust and distrust between social workers and care providers

Risk work is dependent on social relations between individuals and organisations. Trust forms an important part of this. Brown and Calnan note that the issue of trust becomes relevant 'when there is an awareness of the potential for negative outcomes as a result of acting in relation to and relying upon another' (2012, p 18). From the perspective of social workers, they needed to decide how far they could trust the accounts of care providers. Social workers identified several factors as influencing their views on this.

First, social workers referred to CQC inspection reports to assess the quality of a provider. The CQC is the independent regulator of health and social care in England and has a role in registering care providers and in monitoring, inspecting and rating services (CQC, 2022).[1] Some social workers would contact the CQC where their inspection reports indicated poor practice or where the inspection was ongoing. Trust in providers was also informed by informal knowledge within the team. For example, Kerry was unable to get through to a member of staff on the telephone at one care home. She displayed her frustration by making comments to other social workers in the office, such as "Lodge House are shit" and "don't ever go to Lodge House" (from field notes). While opinions about providers were not always voiced so vociferously, casual conversations among team members led to a shared knowledge as to who were the 'good' and 'bad' providers. Where concerns about the reputation of a care provider were held from either source of knowledge, social workers began enquiries from a position of distrust. Consequently, they would require a higher degree of evidence from the care providers in question compared to those with positive reputations. Such reputations about care providers were not static and could be observed to change over time. This was illustrated by Kerry: "I always have this theory that it's like the captain of the ship, or the headmaster, sort of. If you've got someone who is really strong and has the vision at the top or within that setting, I think it bodes well" (From interview). This view about leadership was common. While a care provider or a care home might be viewed as having provided poor care previously, social workers tended to be more trusting of care providers where new managers were seen to be making efforts to turn the agency around.

The second factor that influenced social workers' trust in care homes was the way the homes engaged with social workers. Where safeguarding concerns were reported, social workers expected to speak to a manager or a deputy manager. For example, Jenny reflected on the difficulties she had locating a manager. She said:

'it's just that it raises doubts in your own mind. Why can't I contact the manager? Why aren't we having this information? We are not reassured that the risks are being managed, and there's been quite a lot of turnover of management in that home ... to the point where now I don't even know for certain who the manager is.' (From interview)

This lack of availability was viewed with suspicion on the basis that it indicated defensiveness or understaffing, both viewed as potential risk factors for poor care. By contrast, social workers indicated that they were reassured by managers who made themselves available to talk, did not minimise safeguarding concerns and were open to suggestions about how to manage it.

Third, social workers trusted care providers who showed a good understanding of the safeguarding process and what was required to assuage concerns. For example, Kerry acknowledged that it was important to have respect for care providers, though this was qualified with "but I expect them to be saying things that I would find reassuring" (from interview). The safeguarding process was complex and based on unstated expectations by social workers, not just direct observance of law or policy. Specifically, social workers expected care providers to provide reassurance around safeguarding concerns through documentary evidence – mainly care plans and risk assessments. Care providers who were proactive in providing such documentation and showing how any concerns had been addressed were trusted. Social workers distrusted providers who were unable to provide such paperwork. Some social workers noted a problem with this. For example, Penny said, "I'm not entire[ly] sure if the providers know exactly what we're after" (from interview), and she suggested that the local authority needed to provide standardised paperwork and training on how to complete it. By contrast, others argued that it was important not to explain the process. For example, Kerry said:

'Because what I don't want to do is phone up a provider and lead them through the yes(es) and no(s). … But [if] I phone up and say have you done your care plan?, have you done your risk assessment?, have you done this?, they're just going to answer yes to everything in my mind, and then they're going to run off and do it as we've finished the phone call, if they're going to do that.' (From interview)

While Kerry justified her practice on the basis that it might lead to disguised compliance, it reflected a lack of thought among some social workers as to how care providers might come to a position where they understood their expectations around the safeguarding process.

Asking care agencies to reflect on their responsibility

When thinking about how risk work is conducted, it is important to consider the issue of where responsibility lies (Gale et al, 2016). As we saw earlier in this chapter, risk assessments were seen to identify where service users should be enabled to take risks in their own lives and which agencies should be responsible for managing these. This showed that risk assessment and care planning documents were used to assign responsibility to a range of workers in the care sector, such as care workers or housing support workers. However, where care agencies were suspected to be responsible for risks to service users, the concept of responsibility was deployed in different ways.

In cases where safeguarding concerns which the social worker believed were potentially serious were received, the social worker could request that the care provider conduct an internal investigation. This was presented as a fact-finding mission in which care providers were asked to gather information and report back, but it was also concerned with identifying how agencies should be held responsible. Requests to conduct an internal investigation came with an element of threat. For example, Nicola said: "we will contact them today and say have you got care plans in place? Have you updated risk assessments? How are you managing this concern? The only way you are going to do it [is to] do an internal investigation as soon as possible" (From interview).

Nicola's insistence that, "the only way you are going to do it [is to] do an internal investigation" reflects the use of professional authority. Care providers were being told rather than asked to conduct an enquiry. Additionally, the presentation of internal investigations as fact-finding missions was not always honest. In several cases, social workers had already conducted their own enquiries and decided that the care agencies were responsible. For example, Lisa conducted an enquiry in which a nurse reported a service user having a cut on his arm. The man in question had told the nurse that the carers had been a "bit rough" with him. When contacted initially, the care agency said that the cut had occurred because of skin irritation from a jumper, which did not tally with the account they had originally provided to the nurse. Lisa justified the internal investigation in the following terms:

Lisa: Can the agency come to terms with what's happened?
Jeremy: OK.
Lisa: Can they look at that risk of what happened, of that incident, you know, and while the staff could not report it, you know, can they look at that and can they, you know, develop up a culture of trust and better awareness. It's an accident, why couldn't they, you know ... so if I can get that from speaking to the care coordinators there ...
Jeremy: Yes.
Lisa: And [if] I get the sense it's going forward, you know, that they can report, it's not ... why didn't they report it? [It] is their fear, cultural fear, you know ... I mustn't report it, you know ...
Jeremy: Yes.

Lisa: ... and make up a story that it was an itchy jumper – was it ... or are we talking about a different arm or different person?

Lisa made it clear within the interview that she believed the carers had not been telling the truth about the incident in question. The purpose of the internal investigation, from her perspective, was to enable the agency to "come to terms with what's happened" and to reflect on how they should react were a similar incident to occur in the future. In doing so, care providers were being asked to reflect on their responsibility, with Lisa indicating later in the interview that she would not proceed to a "full-blown" safeguarding enquiry if the agency admitted fault. Similarly, social workers might give agencies tasks to complete within strategy meetings, such as updating policies and procedures relating to the risk issue at question (such as fall prevention). In other words, agencies were commonly given tasks in which they could reflect on their responsibilities as a means of preventing abuse in the future.

In exceptional cases, social workers highlighted the limitations of encouraging care agencies to reflect on their responsibilities, on the basis that this underplayed the local authorities' responsibilities in funding appropriate care. Patricia reflected on changes in her own practice. She told me that in the past she used to go "straight to the jugular of the care home", but had since come to be more circumspect. For example:

Patricia: So we got ourselves into a rut that care homes are just this ... and we are only going to pay them six hundred quid or seven hundred quid ... and you do everything from someone who can wash and dress and is no problem at all to someone who is incredibly high end and [we] will just give you an extra hundred pounds for your efforts?

Jeremy: Yes.

Patricia: So I am not dismissing that there are a lot of serious safeguarding cases. What I am saying is that we need to really re-look rather than keep patching up, patching up, patching up, patching up.

Jeremy: Yes.

Patricia: Does that makes sense to you?

Jeremy: Yes, it does.

Patricia: And I think it's a policy thing or a commissioning, much bigger commissioning thing, because you squeeze here and it's going to come up here. It has to, because it's the same resource.

Jeremy: Yes.

Patricia: So, if now my Mrs C needs a lot of help, Mr D is not going to get that help.

Jeremy: Yes, yes.

Patricia: I'm sorry but Mr D's going to be our next safeguarding.

In Patricia's account, attention was paid to the funding and commissioning limitations which affected how care workers and care providers were able to respond. This was seen to lead to recurrent safeguarding referrals due to inadequate resources being directed from one resident to another. These observations had implications for how Patricia dealt with cases. First, it was seen as important to assess how far individual or agency practice was responsible for the risks presented, rather than ignoring the question about the impacts of resourcing. Second, it was a way to use safeguarding enquiries or strategy meetings to draw in broader resources from the local authority or health services. These interventions were then seen as means through which the local authority and health services might work together with social care providers to meet their responsibility to the service user concerned.

Conclusion

This chapter focused on the way in which social workers engage with service users and carers. It identified that risk assessments are an important intervention, but do not drive practice to the extent suggested in existing literature (Webb, 2006; Green, 2007; Pollack, 2010). My research found that not all social workers were aware of the risk assessments within their own local authorities. No social workers referred to risk assessment practices being driven by research or statistics. Rather, risk assessments were informed by social workers' perceptions of the safeguarding principles (DHSC, 2022) as well as by the views of other professionals and service users. A key function of risk assessment tools was to record the tolerability of risk and indicate what actions should be taken, if any. There has been much debate within the risk literature about how concepts of risk and responsibility are balanced within risk work (Ferguson, 2007; Raitakari et al, 2019). Risk assessment tools were used to record where service users should be enabled to take positive risks, and to combat paternalistic decision-making. In doing so, they documented where care agencies should retain the responsibility for managing risks and at what point future risks could be viewed as a safeguarding concern.

Risk work involves drawing on knowledge about risk and intervening to manage it. Adult safeguarding law and policy identifies service user involvement as central to this process (Care Act, 2014; DHSC, 2022; LGA, 2022b). Social workers were keen to champion these principles but highlighted several tensions in practice. Current law and policy offer few pointers as to how social workers should respond in urgent situations. When conducting safeguarding enquiries, social workers sought to assess whether the person was in immediate danger. Where this was the case, social workers sometimes took actions to ensure their safety before seeking their views. Further tensions existed due to the remote nature of safeguarding work, with many social workers being tasked with conducting enquiries by telephone. Here, the need for a more nuanced assessment caused some workers to refer the enquiry to other social workers who could meet the service user face to face, although these decisions might cause delays. Social workers also highlighted tensions with the policy ideal of service users as 'rational actors' (Kemshall, 2010), keen to engage in discussions about risk. These narratives overlooked difficulties in the social relations between social workers and the public, in which individuals may have little incentive to engage with a safeguarding enquiry. Lastly, the weight of referrals also meant that social workers needed to make pragmatic decisions about whether they could afford the time to engage with service users where the information had been provided by others.

Work with service users was concerned with translating legal knowledge and establishing trusting relationships. This was then used to educate service users about abuse and neglect and how they could access help. Most social workers emphasised the need to build trust with family carers. When building social relations with this group, social workers either downplayed their authority to build trust or set out the carer's responsibilities in a more assertive approach. Trust was also an important issue where social workers were working with care agencies, though in these cases the focus was on whether care agencies could be trusted. Various sources of risk knowledge were used to inform these judgements, including CQC reports, team knowledge and assessment of the way care providers engaged with the process. Interventions largely focused on requiring care homes to provide documentary evidence as a way to emphasise their responsibilities to report safeguarding concerns to the local authority.

Conclusion

Risk work within adult safeguarding practice

In this book, I have drawn on theories of risk work to consider how social workers understand and manage risk. The issue of risk is central to adult safeguarding with current law and policy focusing on 'safeguarding adults at risk of abuse or neglect'. However, little attention has been given to the way the concept of risk is understood and deployed by social workers when doing adult safeguarding work. Previous research has used the framework of risk work to examine adult safeguarding (Robb and McCarthy, 2023), though this research focuses specifically on safeguarding people with learning disabilities. The remit of my research was wider and examined safeguarding decisions across all adult groups. Drawing on theories of risk work, this book has focused on the interactions between risk knowledge, interventions and social relations (Brown and Gale, 2018a, 2018b). It has also considered how social workers seek to balance these key features and the tensions which occur between them.

This concluding chapter aims to do two things. In the first section, I examine what the research tells us theoretically about risk. Here, I show how my theories compare to those of previous social work academics and what this research tells us that is new. In the second section, I turn to the issue of policy and practice to explore what changes should be made.

Risk and social work revisited

Many social work authors have drawn on Beck's assertion that risk has replaced need in contemporary society to argue that risk has replaced need in social work practice (Alfandari et al, 2023). The concept of risk is largely seen in negative terms in the critical social work literature. Risk is seen to shift the focus away from present need to a concern about what *might* happen in the future (Webb, 2006; Green, 2007). This is seen as altering the focus of social work practice, which becomes concerned with future risks over current needs. These policy responses are also seen as promoting neoliberal notions of choice by considering which service users are encouraged to assess and manage risks in their own lives, and this is associated with the withdrawal of state services (Kemshall, 2016). Furthermore, it is argued that social worker interventions become framed by statistical information, which neglects the voice of individual service users (Webb, 2009).

The concept of risk work (Horlick-Jones, 2005; Brown and Gale, 2018a, 2018b) is useful as it has the potential to challenge grand theories of risk and identify how risk is understood and used on the ground. My research challenges current social work thinking about risk in several ways. I highlight these under the headings of risk knowledge, interventions, and social relations.

Risk knowledge

A central argument within the critical social work literature is that risk thinking has overridden other forms of social work knowledge (Kemshall et al, 1997; Webb, 2006; Green, 2007). While some critics argue that risk might be viewed positively and point to the problem of seeing care and control in dichotomous terms (Kemshall et al, 2013; Hardy, 2015), these writers tend to be in the minority.

There are serious problems with viewing risk in wholly negative terms, as much of the critical literature does. As Horlick-Jones recognises, the term 'risk' can be deployed in many ways, often simultaneously (see Alaszewski, 2018). It is therefore possible that some of these framings of risk are helpful while others are unhelpful. To examine this issue properly, we first need to consider how the term is used in policy before considering how the social workers in this study applied it in practice. Chapter 1 of this book showed how awareness of adult abuse and neglect in England has evolved. Despite recognition of child abuse as a social problem in the 1970s (Parton, 1979), recognition of adult abuse and neglect was slow to materialise, despite the efforts of activist groups as well as some practitioners and academics. Law and policy was also slow to evolve despite public scandals. However, an awareness of the problem of adult abuse did develop, with *No Secrets* (Department of Health, 2000) and the Care Act 2014 being milestones. The Care Act 2014 focuses on 'safeguarding adults at risk of abuse and neglect' (see Sections 42–47) and has also promoted new care standards in response to failings within the health and social care system. This recognition of adult abuse and neglect was hard won by activists and should be seen as a step forward in upholding the human rights of all adults. Current law and guidance do not suggest that considerations of risk should override all other concerns. Rather, they state that practitioners should consider the context of abuse and neglect, and how this relates to the person's needs for care and support as well as the person's wellbeing (see Dixon, 2021).

If we are to address the criticism that risk thinking dominates social work practice, we also need to examine how such knowledge is used. In line with previous safeguarding research, my study found that legal and policy knowledge was core to risk work within adult safeguarding (Stevenson and Taylor, 2017; Stevens et al, 2018). This did not mean that social workers were passive recipients of law and policy. Social workers recognised the safeguarding risks which adults might experience and saw assessing these risks as an important part of their role. The Care Act 2014 was welcomed because it provided social workers with statutory powers to manage such risks and acted to improve multi–agency engagement. Section 42 of the Care Act 2014, the *Care and Support Statutory Guidance* (DHSC, 2022) and the Mental Capacity Act 2005 were key sources of knowledge to guide interventions around the management of risk. Legal and policy frameworks were used to define which individuals safeguarding duties applied to and the categories of abuse. Zinn (2008) notes that policy debates often frame problems and solutions in ideal terms in which rational strategies for managing risk (drawing on scientific or technical knowledge) are preferred to nonrational strategies. Social workers in my study made distinctions between ideal notions of practice (in which legal and policy measures could be neatly applied) and the messier realities of risk work. In doing this, they highlighted several limitations of the law and policies which were central to their risk knowledge. Section 42 of the Care Act 2014 was seen to be key to making decisions around safeguarding, though the criteria was viewed as "woolly". Social workers felt more confident in making decisions where they had interventions in the shape of tools to guide them, and they appreciated tools which helped them to judge whether categories of risk, such as self–neglect or hoarding, were met. They were, however, suspicious of tools whose goals were to ration resources.

Commentators have argued that the Care Act 2014 has the potential to improve safeguarding practice through its focus on the wellbeing of individuals, the outcomes they wish to achieve and the way in which they want the process to be managed (Cooper and Bruin, 2017). Social workers were supportive of this view but highlighted problems in applying the principles of the Care Act 2014 to practice. The biggest challenge was austerity. In line with research elsewhere (Forrester-Jones et al, 2020; Marczak et al, 2022), social workers described local authorities as being under intense funding pressures, causing them to reduce their services. Because of this, legal and policy knowledge was often reformulated by social workers to re–establish who should provide care in what circumstances. This was problematic and is discussed in more detail later.

As already mentioned, a concern among social work risk theorists is that policies have come to draw on neoliberal narratives of service user choice (Webb, 2006), a concern which has also been expressed in relation to the personalisation agenda (Scourfield, 2010; Carey, 2022). This policy framing has been seen by critics as compromising social work thinking and practice. These criticisms were partially upheld by my research findings. Social work accounts were heavily influenced by the personalisation agenda and by the Making Safeguarding Personal initiative. Workers echoed policy narratives that personalisation policies (HM Government, 2007; Department of Health, 2011) were the antidote to paternalism and that they should focus on facilitating service user choice in an often uncritical way. The concept of choice is often viewed by social work academics as problematic on the basis that it is used to promote free market ideals, which undermine the universal provision of service (Scourfield, 2010; Carey, 2022). However, it is important to note that social workers' readings of choice were not limited, in the way that critics suggest, to pursuing such ideals. The concept of choice used by social workers in this study did identify what types of services individuals could purchase, but it was also used more broadly than this. Commonly, the term was used to acknowledge that individuals had the right to make decisions on their own behalf. In other words, social workers were using it to combat discriminatory views among providers that certain types of people (such as older people, people with learning disabilities or people with addiction issues) should not be allowed to take decisions in their own lives. In these instances, the term 'choice' was used to highlight the autonomy of service users, in line with the positive risk taking literature (Robertson and Collinson, 2011; Titterton, 2011), rather than being used purely as a means to encourage them to take responsibility for their for their own welfare.

A further concern among social work theorists has been that ICT systems prioritise risk thinking, with concepts such as 'risk' and 'need' coming to be viewed as binary categories with an emphasis on increasing service efficiency (Webb, 2006; Parton, 2008; Rogowski, 2011; Harris, 2022). Within my research, ICT systems were seen as a key source of risk knowledge, as they held historical records of previous risks, which were used to inform decision-making. They also aided interventions in the sense that they highlighted which referrals were seen as urgent or otherwise. However, social workers rarely complained about ICT systems limiting their thinking. The key problem identified by social workers was that the ICT systems were not efficient enough, being difficult to navigate and containing incomplete information. Social workers conducting assessments were obliged to draw on records from the ICT system, but this knowledge was seen as incomplete and piecemeal. They therefore had to engage in a process of translating risks (Gale et al, 2016). Risk work involved making sense of the pieces of information available, with the assessment process being used to draw together past information and collect information in the future. The process of building a picture was seen as core to adult safeguarding work. Social workers drew on multiple sources of information to identify potential risks, with further work being conducted to identify whether such risks were present. Social relations, in the form of team cultures, were also central to social workers' risk work. It was a common expectation within teams that social workers should be looking for patterns of risk over time within referral information and ICT systems. When judging whether individual cases met the threshold for intervention, social workers tended to look to their peers to try to ensure that decision-making was consistent within teams.

Interventions

A contention among social work theorists is that forms of risk thinking, baked into ICT systems or standardised procedures, come to drive the assessment and management of risk by social workers (Webb, 2006; Parton, 2008; Sletten and Ellingsen, 2020; Harris, 2022). For example, Webb expresses concern about 'the hardening of technical planning and ... the rational orchestration of procedural rules for practice governance' (2006, pp 168–69). These trends are seen as concerning because they limit social work discretion and compromise social work values. My findings indicate that systems encouraging practitioners to consider risk did exist, but that these did not limit social work discretion in the ways that have been claimed. Within my research, several policies and procedures were applied by each local authority to influence the way risk work was conducted. As well as being used as a source of risk knowledge, ICT systems were used in all local authorities to structure safeguarding work and to identify which assessments should be prioritised. Interventions used in Fosborough were designed to draw distinctions between short-term safeguarding work, which could be done from the office, and longer-term safeguarding work, which was conducted by adult community teams. From a governmentality perspective, these interventions can be understood as 'technologies of government' designed to shape social workers' thinking and action (Castel, 1991). However, as some governmentality theorists note, policy is not totalising and individuals have the power to resist (McKee, 2009). Social workers in my study accepted the premise that ICT systems should be used to prioritise assessments. They also accepted the divisions of labour between safeguarding teams and adult community teams in their local authority. However, these bureaucratic systems were seen to have limitations. ICT systems were not useful for prioritising large numbers of referrals and so individual workers and teams devised their own systems to manage them. In other words, a range of informal measures were sanctioned by managers within teams. These are similar to the 'informal logics of risk' seen in child protection, in which values formed within teams are used to alter or adapt national or local policies (Broadhurst et al, 2010).

Another contention which has been made by social work academics is that risk assessments have come to drive social work practice (see Hardy, 2017) and draw heavily on the logics of actuarialism (Webb, 2006, 2009). This was not the case in my study. No social workers reported that they were using risk assessments drawing on statistical data. Rather than being based on actuarial knowledge, these tools were seen as reflecting certain values within health and social care, namely that risk should be discussed within multidisciplinary meetings and that it was useful to record a chronology of risk. These interventions were used to emphasise where state responsibilities lay. However, this was not done purely to limit state resources, as responsibilisation theories suggest (O' Malley, 2009). These interventions indicated when service users should be enabled to engage in positive risk taking or permitted to make unwise decisions. In making this decision, social workers indicated where service users were able to take risks, in line with the principles of the Mental Capacity Act 2005 and positive risk taking (Titterton, 2011). However, there was an implicit assumption that care agencies who were supporting service users should continue to monitor and manage risks and should support positive risk taking where possible. Rather than this being a process through which service users were responsibilised for risk taking, it was instead a process through which external agencies were made responsible for the management of risk, through risk assessment and care planning documents, a point which is discussed later in this chapter.

While my findings do not support some of the common assertions in the social work risk literature, this should not be taken to mean that the management of adult safeguarding risk was unproblematic. While social workers felt that different teams were able to adapt local procedures, they also highlighted shortcomings with safeguarding interventions. These shortcomings were not viewed as inevitable by social workers, but were seen to arise due to increased demands and reduced resources. Because of these demands, social workers indicated that safeguarding interventions were becoming increasingly compromised.

Systems for managing risks within health and care systems are often predicated on an ideal model which can be understood as a 'risk escalator' (Heyman et al, 2004). In other words, models are designed on the basis that more resources should be provided at the top end of the systems where the risk is high, and less resources at the bottom ends of the system where the risk is low. However, blockages may occur in the system, challenging ideals of practice. These problems were evident in safeguarding work and impacted on safeguarding practices in several ways. First, social workers indicated that austerity had led to a reduction in health and social care services in the statutory, voluntary and private sectors. Because of this, safeguarding was viewed as "the last stop", which led to an increase in both the number of safeguarding referrals and the complexity of safeguarding work. Second, social workers reported that safeguarding systems often did not work as intended due to shortage of experienced workers. Third, such shortages reduced the quality of safeguarding work, with social workers struggling to find time to engage with care providers or only being able to work with service users in a limited way to prevent abuse.

These problems affected the way social workers interpreted the principles of safeguarding, with the principles primarily being used to facilitate a movement of cases through the system. It was particularly notable that the principle of proportionality was used more than other principles. The term 'proportionality' was used to denote cases in which the local authority should not intervene, to identify where safeguarding workers might use a lighter touch or to show where responses by other agencies had been adequate. Social workers also used the term 'accountability' differently from the way it was used in policy, emphasising concerns about blame and ways in which it could be mitigated. However, it would be wrong to state that these principles were purely used to promote efficiency or mitigate blame. The terms 'partnership' and 'prevention' were used positively to talk about ways local authorities might work with providers to avert future abuse occurring, with 'prevention' also used in relation to actions which might help service users feel safe. Other principles were notable by their absence. The principles of wellbeing, protection and empowerment were rarely referenced by social workers, although they did speak more broadly about actions which had been taken to avert risk or to involve service users in decision-making.

Social relations

Theoretical work focusing on the management of risk in social work has little to say about how social workers manage social relations when doing risk work. As Kemshall notes, proceduralism and managerialism have been seen to result 'in a focus on monitoring and information exchange at the expense of understanding, problem solving and client engagement' (2010, p 1255). Such changes are seen as taking place to the annoyance of front-line staff who view computer-based work as having replaced relationship-based practice (Harris, 2022). However, more recent research has partially challenged this view by identifying that while risk is managed through process and bureaucracy, building trusting relationships is seen by social workers as key to this work (Robb and McCarthy, 2023). My research also indicates that social workers see relationship-based work as central to assessing risk. Social workers were supportive in principle of the policy aim that safeguarding should be person-centred, and they saw themselves as championing this. Where contact with service users could be established, social workers saw good social relations between themselves and the service users as central to the work. Nonetheless, practical problems were seen to exist. Social workers felt the need to prioritise service users' immediate safety before talking to them about their wishes. Service users often chose to avoid contact with social services and were reluctant to engage in risk work. Also interviews focusing on service user wishes were difficult to conduct by telephone. When working with service users, social workers identified several actions which were important for establishing trust. These included being candid about the legal nature of the work and providing simplified explanations or analogies to explain the safeguarding task. Risk work also involved defending service users' rights to take positive risks. In line with Robb and McCarthy's (2023) research and other adult safeguarding research, several social workers indicated that they viewed social relations as the central axis of risk work. Such work was seen as relying on empathy for the service user, but also as requiring a clear explanation of safeguarding, which involved knowledge translation. As the law is central to risk decision-making in safeguarding, social workers were concerned with giving lay explanations. This was balanced against duties to explain the nature of abuse and neglect and to educate service users as to how they could access support in the future.

Safeguarding research conducted prior to the introduction of the Care Act 2014 reported strained social relations between social workers and other agencies (McCreadie et al, 2008). Social workers' accounts in this research indicate that different agencies continued to interpret statutory criteria differently to them since the introduction of the Care Act 2014. When assessing safeguarding referrals, social workers were not only trying to assess the information they had received but also the referrers' motivations. A major theme which emerged was that of dealing with 'inappropriate referrals'. Here, social workers highlighted a range of concerns which were seen not to meet the safeguarding criteria. In many cases, professionals were seen to have flagged up a general care need without identifying other elements of the criteria in Section 42 of the Care Act 2014. These referrals were seen to be motivated by a concern that 'something needs to be done' or by defensive decision-making by other professionals. Additionally, social workers believed that some professionals used the safeguarding system cynically to try and 'game the system' to access care for a person more quickly. Cultural beliefs about what other services' thought were therefore an important starting point in risk work decisions. Views as to how these social relations should be managed varied. On the one hand, social workers believed that the local authority should be educating referrers about the Care Act 2014 with a view to reducing inappropriate referrals. On the other hand, they believed that efforts should be taken to encourage referrals, because this would allow risks (which may or may not meet the criteria for safeguarding) to be tracked over time.

Previous research has indicated that maintaining trust and communicating risks diplomatically are important elements in establishing social relations during risk work (Brown and Calnan, 2012; Gale et al, 2017) and social work (Pithouse et al, 2012). The issue of trust was highlighted when working with family carers. In the case of care agencies, social workers tended to downplay safeguarding law and policy and highlight other knowledge, emphasising support to carers. In exceptional cases, social workers took a more assertive approach by identifying carers' responsibilities within law. The theme of trust was also dominant when social workers were working with care agencies. However, in these cases, workers tended to place strong emphasis on the responsibilities of care agencies. Social workers drew on both institutional knowledge, in the shape of CQC reports, and team knowledge of care homes' practice to identify whether specific providers were trustworthy or not. Asking care providers to complete internal investigations was also used to highlight responsibility. In exceptional cases, social workers talked of the need for more equitable social relationships with care providers, drawing on knowledge of how austerity policies effected their ability to provide care. These dynamics were a problematic part of social work practice and I talk about this in more detail in the next section.

Future issues for policy and practice

In this final section, I reflect on the implications of my research for future adult safeguarding law, policy and practice. Before I do so, I would like to return to the issue of how social problems come to be seen and their subsequent development. Best (2013) argues that once governments have introduced policy agendas, professionals then engage in social problem work to implement these policies. A final stage may then occur in which individuals raise problems with the current system and call for changes to be made. This leads me to consider where the social work profession currently stands within this. My research has identified mixed feelings among social workers about adult safeguarding practice and the management of risk within it. What does this tell us about what should be done in the future?

The Care Act 2014 was significant because it made safeguarding a statutory duty for the first time. Social workers in the study appreciated the increased status that the Act had given to safeguarding, but reported difficulties interpreting the law. However, they felt that there was a lack of clarity around the categories of abuse contained in the *Care and Support Statutory Guidance* (DHSC, 2022). This criticism echoes that of legal commentators (Fitzgerald, 2016; Clements, 2018) and safeguarding adults reviews (Preston-Shoot, 2018). For example, standard definitions of self-neglect are yet to be agreed, and it is unclear whether some categories of abuse (such as hoarding) are intended to be distinct or subcategories of others. Revisions of the statutory guidance should provide more detailed criteria for practitioners. There is also a need for Safeguarding Adults Boards in local authorities to provide guidance and training to social workers in their area. A substantial amount of research has been done on the topic of self-neglect since my research was undertaken (Preston-Shoot, 2019, 2020; Preston-Shoot et al, 2022), and there is potential for this work to inform policy and practice.

A dominant theme among the social workers in my study was the effects of austerity on their day-to-day work with service users. These effects are well documented. Figures show that the spending power of local authorities reduced by 30 per cent between 2010 and 2018 (Rex and Campbell, 2022). Previous discussions have acknowledged that austerity policies have a negative effect on local authorities' ability to promote personalisation and choice as intended (Lymbery, 2014). However, criticisms of the Care Act 2014 have tended to focus on the limitations of the legislation itself (such as, the lack of detail on how new legal powers should be exercised; Marczak et al, 2022). My research shows that local authorities have struggled to keep up with the rising level of safeguarding referrals. While practitioners welcomed the growing awareness of adult abuse and neglect, they indicated that their systems were struggling to meet the rising demands. These problems were compounded by more cases becoming safeguarding concerns due to the increased rationing of health and social care services. The work needed to combat this problem needs to be addressed through general political engagement rather than the actions of individual social workers. However, leaders within the profession will need to engage in lobbying for such changes.

My research revealed troubling findings about how the principles of safeguarding were interpreted by some social workers. As stated earlier, the principle of proportionality was used most frequently, primarily to reject referrals. While social workers do need to exercise discretion as to which referrals are accepted or rejected, the principles were used flexibly with a view to keeping referral levels down. Much of the social work risk literature assumes that such practices are driven by statistics and managerialism. However, I saw little evidence of this. Rather, teams appeared to agree informal thresholds among themselves to keep the system moving. What is the answer to this? A common response within the social work literature is that we should challenge poor practices by 'going back to our values'. However, this response is inadequate, as social work values can be applied subjectively (as evidenced by my research findings). In my view, these issues can only be resolved through careful consideration of the ethics of safeguarding. One way to do this is through closer consideration of how national legislation can be aligned with international human rights frameworks such as the United Nations Convention on the Rights of Persons with Disabilities (Dixon et al, 2022). However, such work is at an early stage and requires future development.

Previous inquiries have highlighted the detrimental effects on service users and their families where care agencies fail (Manthorpe and Martineau, 2015). Social workers in Gainsborough raised challenges which had occurred through a recent failure of a care agency and the potential failure of another. While social workers were aware that service users were at risk due to the possibility of a provider failing, social workers were unsure of how to manage this situation due to the provider being unwilling or unable to respond to safeguarding measures. Sections 48–52 of the Care Act 2014 identify the steps which should be taken in the event of provider failure, including a temporary duty on local authorities to provide care where a regulated provider becomes unable to carry out an activity due to business failure. Previous research indicates that provider failure is high, with 77 per cent of councils surveyed in 2015 saying that a failure of at least one provider had taken place in the past year (Koehler, 2015). Local authorities should have business and contingency plans in place to manage such events (Koehler, 2015). There is a need for such plans to indicate how these decisions will be communicated to safeguarding workers and what interim measures should be taken to manage any allegations of abuse or neglect.

Future research and policy should explore the challenges in engaging people with adult safeguarding. So far, this issue has been unacknowledged. For example, a systematic review of qualitative research on Making Safeguarding Personal (Ahuja et al, 2022) listed only one study which mentioned that service users may not wish to engage with the process. In this case, the study reported that not all adults referred for safeguarding wanted, or were able to, engage without an advocate (Hertfordshire Safeguarding Adults Board, 2017). While the LGA's *Making Safeguarding Personal Toolkit* (LGA, 2022b) provides useful resources – particularly in areas such as advocacy, jargon busting and family group conferencing – these tend to assume that individuals are keen to engage in discussions around their safety. This is clearly not the case. Future research should be commissioned to discover service users' attitudes towards safeguarding adults enquiries, and this should be used to inform future policy.

There has been a recognition within the child safeguarding literature that child protection practices have focused unduly on the control of parents while offering them insufficient support (Featherstone et al, 2019). This issue is relevant to work with service users, carers and care providers. Social workers in my study were aware of the need to support service users and family carers, but tended not to consider support which may be required by care providers, seeing changes in practice as being wholly their responsibility. Inquiry reports do show that staff in hospitals and care homes have the potential to be neglectful or sadistic, and this needs to be addressed. However, research also shows that many behaviours which can be experienced as abusive or neglectful come about where care workers lack training (Cooper et al, 2013). Most care workers are not highly qualified. Expecting homes to have a detailed understanding of legal and policy frameworks shows a lack of imagination and empathy. There was an attitude among social workers that safeguarding practice should rely heavily on asking care providers to provide paperwork. While care homes should be required to document key decisions carefully, there is no evidence that these processes prevent abuse or neglect. Furthermore such regulatory procedures now dominate care home practice, challenging providers' ability to provide good care to their residents (Teggi, 2022). This issue requires further attention by local authorities involved in commissioning care services.

Safeguarding adults at risk of abuse and neglect is still a relatively new area of social work practice. Increased attention to adult safeguarding practice should be welcomed. The Care Act 2014 should be seen as a step forward in the recognition of the problem of adult abuse and neglect. However, the measures contained in the Care Act 2014 do not go far enough. While the *Care and Support Statutory Guidance* (DHSC, 2022) has introduced new categories of abuse, current guidance remains ambiguous to social workers and difficult to decipher. Better guidance and tools should be developed to guide social workers in this regard, although not at the expense of professional discretion. If the safeguarding system is to be effective, it needs to be properly funded. Continued activism and advocacy is needed to identify the strain that the system is currently under and to identify solutions which allow social workers to spend an adequate amount of time with those with care and support needs who are subject to or at risk of abuse and neglect. Lastly, more discussion around the ethics of safeguarding is needed so that there is more agreement within the profession as to how we can ensure the principles of social justice are central to adult safeguarding work.

Notes

Chapter 1

[1] The Law Commission is a government-commissioned independent body responsible for reviewing English law and suggesting policy change.

[2] The document referred to the National Assistance Act 1948 and the Mental Health Act 1983. Section 47 of the National Assistance Act 1948 allowed for the 'removal to suitable premises of persons in need of care and attention'. This needed to be authorised by a magistrate and could be used for those who were seriously ill, living in squalor or not receiving proper care and attention. The Mental Health Act 1983 (as amended by the Mental Health Act 2007) allows for people with a mental disorder to be detained and assessed or treated in hospital where the conditions in the legislation are met.

[3] Research focusing on how *No Secrets* was applied is set out in greater detail in the next chapter, focusing on social workers understand and manage risk.

[4] This falls under Regulation 20 of the Health and Social Care Act 2008 (Regulated Activities) Regulations 2014. See Kelly and Quick (2019) for further details. The Care Quality Commission (Registration) Regulations 2009 also state that providers must report specific harms to the CQC, including abuse or allegations of abuse.

Chapter 3

[1] As noted in Chapter 1, the guidance lists several types of abuse: physical abuse, domestic violence, sexual abuse, psychological abuse, financial or material abuse, modern slavery, discriminatory abuse, organisational abuse, neglect and acts of omission, self-neglect, domestic abuse and financial abuse (DHSC, 2022, para 14.17). This list is not intended to be exhaustive and other types of abuse or neglect may be considered.

[2] The use of the term 'threshold' was omitted from LGA guidance in 2018. This change was made 'to avoid any inference that an individual must "pass a test" or "reach a threshold" to get safeguarding support' (LGA, 2019, p 6).

Chapter 4

[1] Current guidance states that the concept of wellbeing should be applied broadly (DHSC, 2022, para 1.5). Section 1(2) of the Care Act 2014 states that wellbeing relates to any of the following: '(a) personal dignity (including treating of the individual with respect); (b) physical and mental health and emotional well-being; (c) protection from abuse and neglect; (d) control by the individual over day-to-day life (including over care and support, or support, provided to the individual and the way in which it is provided); (e) participation in work, education, training or recreation; (f) social and economic well-being; (g) domestic, family and personal relationships; (h) suitability of living accommodation; (i) the individual's contribution to society.'

[2] Section 1(3(b)) of the Care Act 2014 states that local authorities must give regard to 'the individual's views wishes, feelings and beliefs'. As such, the principle overlaps with the safeguarding principle of empowerment, which is concerned with '[p]eople being supported and encouraged to make their own decisions' with informed consent (DHSC, 2022, para 14.13).

3   An adult's needs meet the eligibility criteria if '(a) the adult's needs arise from or are related to a physical or mental impairment or illness; (b) as a result of the adult's needs the adult is unable to achieve two or more of the outcomes specified in paragraph (2); and (c) as a consequence there is, or is likely to be, a significant impact on the adult's well-being' (The Care and Support (Eligibility Criteria) Regulations 2015, Section 2(1)).

Chapter 5

1   CQC reports rate homes under four different categories. Providers may be rated as 'outstanding', 'good', 'requires improvement' or 'inadequate'.

References

Abbott, S. (2022) 'A study exploring how social work AMHPs experience assessment under mental health law: implications for human rights-oriented social work practice', *The British Journal of Social Work*, 52(3): 1362–79.

ADSS (Association of Directors of Social Services) (2005) *Safeguarding Adults: A National Framework of Standards for Good Practice and Outcomes in Adult Protection Work*, London: ADSS.

Ahuja, L., Price, A., Bramwell, C., Briscoe, S., Shaw, L. and Nunns, M., et al (2022) 'Implementation of the Making Safeguarding Personal approach to strengths-based adult social care: systematic review of qualitative research evidence', *The British Journal of Social Work*, 52(8): 4640–63.

Alaszewski, A. (1999) 'The rise of risk assessment and risk management in the United Kingdom', *International Journal of Public Administration*, 22(3–4): 575–606.

Alaszewski, A. (2018) 'Tom Horlick-Jones and risk work', *Health, Risk & Society*, 20(1–2): 13–22.

Alfandari, R., Taylor, B.J., Baginsky, M., Campbell, J., Helm, D. and Killick, C., et al (2023) 'Making sense of risk: social work at the boundary between care and control', *Health, Risk & Society*, 25(1-2): 75–92.

ARC (Association for Residential Care) and NAPSAC (National Association for the Protection from Sexual Abuse of Adults and Children with Learning Disabilities) (1993) *It Could Never Happen Here: The Prevention and Treatment of Sexual Abuse of Adults with Learning Disabilities in Residential Settings*, Chesterfield/Nottingham: ARC/NAPSAC.

Arnoldi, J. (2009) *Risk*, Cambridge: Polity Press.

Ash, A. (2013) 'A cognitive mask? Camouflaging dilemmas in street-level policy implementation to safeguard older people from abuse', *The British Journal of Social Work*, 43(1): 99–115.

Aspinal, F., Stevens, M., Manthorpe, J., Woolham, J., Samsi, K. and Baxter, K., et al (2019) 'Safeguarding and personal budgets: the experiences of adults at risk', *The Journal of Adult Protection*, 21(3): 157–68.

Baker, A.A. (1981) 'Granny battering', *International Journal of Family Psychiatry*, 2(3–4): 369–78.

Barry, N. (1990) *Welfare*, Buckingham: Open University Press.

Barsky, A. (2015) 'Risks of risk management', *The New Social Worker*. Available from: www.socialworker.com/feature-articles/ethics-articles/risks-of-risk-management/

Bartlett, P. and Sandland, R. (2014) *Mental Health Law: Policy and Practice*, Oxford: Oxford University Press.

BBC (2011) 'Undercover care: the abuse exposed' [TV episode], Panorama.

BBC (2014) 'Staffordshire hospital timeline', 26 February. Available from: www.bbc.co.uk/news/uk-england-stoke-staffordshire-20965469

BBC (2019) 'Stafford Hospital scandal: the real story behind Channel 4's *The Cure*'. Available from: www.bbc.co.uk/news/uk-england-stoke-staffordshire-50836324

Beck, U. (1992) *Risk Society: Towards a New Modernity*, London: Sage.

Beck, U. (1996a) 'Risk society and the provident state', in S. Lash, B. Szerszynski and B. Wynne (eds) *Risk, Environment and Modernity: Towards a New Ecology*, London: Sage, pp 29–43.

Beck, U. (1996b) 'World risk society as cosmopolitan society? Ecological questions in a framework of manufactured uncertainties', *Theory, Culture & Society*, 13(4): 1–32.

Beck, U. (1997) *The Reinvention of Politics: Rethinking Modernity in the Global Social Order* (M. Ritter, trans), Cambridge: Polity.

Beck, U. and Beck-Gernsheim, E. (2002) *Individualization: Institutionalized Individualism and its Social and Political Consequences*, London: Sage.

Beck, U. and Grande, E. (2010) 'Varieties of second modernity: the cosmopolitan turn in social and political theory and research', *The British Journal of Sociology*, 61(3): 409–43.

Beck, U., Bonss, W. and Lau, C. (2003) 'The theory of reflexive modernization: problematic, hypotheses and research programme', *Theory, Culture & Society*, 20(2): 1–33.

Best, J. (2013) *Social Problems* (2nd edn), New York: W.W. Norton & Company.

Bevan, C. (2021) 'Governing "the homeless" in English homelessness legislation: Foucauldian governmentality and the Homelessness Reduction Act 2017', *Housing, Theory and Society*, 38(3): 259–78.

Biggs, S. (1996) 'A family concern: elder abuse in British social policy', *Critical Social Policy*, 16(47): 63–88.

Bittner, E. (1967) 'The police on skid-row: a study of peace keeping', *American Sociological Review*, 32(5): 699–715.

Blumer, H. (1971) 'Social problems as collective behavior', *Social Problems*, 18(3): 298–306.

Booth, K. (2021) 'Critical insurance studies: some geographic directions', *Progress in Human Geography*, 45(5): 1295–310.

Braye, S., Orr, D. and Preston-Shoot, M. (2014) *Self-neglect Policy and Practice: Building an Evidence Base for Adult Social Care*, London: Social Care Institute for Excellence.

Braye, S., Orr, D. and Preston-Shoot, M. (2015) 'Serious case review findings on the challenges of self-neglect: indicators for good practice', *The Journal of Adult Protection*, 17(2): 75–87.

Briggs, M. and Cooper, A. (2018) 'Making Safeguarding Personal: progress of English local authorities', *The Journal of Adult Protection*, 20(1): 59–68.

Broadhurst, K., Hall, C., Wastell, D., White, S. and Pithouse, A. (2010) 'Risk, instrumentalism and the humane project in social work: identifying the informal logics of risk management in children's statutory services', *The British Journal of Social Work*, 40(4): 1046–64.

Brown, H. and Stein, J. (1998) 'Implementing adult protection policies in Kent and East Sussex', *Journal of Social Policy*, 27(3): 371–96.

Brown, L. (2010) 'Balancing risk and innovation to improve social work practice', *The British Journal of Social Work*, 40(4): 1211–28.

Brown, P. and Calnan, M. (2012) *Trusting on the Edge: Managing Uncertainty and Vulnerability in the Midst of Serious Mental Health Problems*, Bristol: Policy Press.

Brown, P. and Gale, N. (2018a) 'Developing a sociology of risk work in client-facing contexts: an editorial', *Health, Risk & Society*, 20(1–2): 1–12.

Brown, P. and Gale, N. (2018b) 'Theorising risk work: analysing professionals' lifeworlds and practices', *Professions and Professionalism*, 8(1): 1–18.

Buckinghamshire County Council (1998) *Independent Longcare Inquiry*, Buckingham: Buckinghamshire County Council.

Burns, D., Hyde, P. and Killett, A. (2013) 'Wicked problems or wicked people? Reconceptualising institutional abuse', *Sociology of Health & Illness*, 35(4): 514–28.

Burrows, D. (2020) *Critical Hospital Social Work*, London: Routledge.

Burston, G.R. (1975) 'Granny-battering', *British Medical Journal*, 3(5983): 592.

Butler, I. and Drakeford, M. (2003) *Social Policy, Social Welfare and Scandal: How British Public Policy is Made*, Basingstoke: Palgrave Macmillan.

Butler, I. and Drakeford, M. (2011) *Social Work on Trial: The Colwell Inquiry and the State of Welfare*, Bristol: Policy Press.

Butler, L. and Manthorpe, J. (2016) 'Putting people at the centre: facilitating Making Safeguarding Personal approaches in the context of the Care Act 2014', *The Journal of Adult Protection*, 18(4): 204–13.

Camden and Islington Community Health Services NHS Trust (1999) *Beech House Inquiry: Report of the Internal Inquiry Relating to the Mistreatment of Patients Residing at Beech House, St Pancras Hospital, during the Period March 1993-April 1996*, London: Camden and Islington Community Health Services NHS Trust.

Canton, R., Littlechild, B. and Fearns, D. (2005) *Risk Assessment and Compliance in Probation and Mental Health Practice*, Lyme Regis: Lyme Regis House Publishing.

Care Act 2014, c 23. Available from: www.legislation.gov.uk/ukpga/2014/23/contents/enacted

Care Standards Act 2000, c 14. Available from: www.legislation.gov.uk/ukpga/2000/14/contents

Carey, M. (2022) 'The neoliberal university, social work and personalised care for older adults', *Ageing & Society*, 42(8): 1964–78.

Carr, S. (2012) *Personalisation: A Rough Guide*, London: Social Care Institute for Excellence.

Castel, R. (1991) 'From dangerousness to risk', in G. Burchell, C. Gordon and P. Miller (eds) *The Foucault Effect: Studies in Governmentality*, Chicago: University of Chicago Press, pp 281–98.

Clements, L. (2018) 'Care Act 2014: overview guide'. Available from: http://www.lukeclements.co.uk/resources/care-act-2014-overview-guide/

Cohen, I. (2006) 'Modernity', in B.S. Turner (ed) *The Cambridge Dictionary of Sociology*, Cambridge: Cambridge University Press, pp 389–94.

Cooper, A. and Bruin, C. (2017) 'Adult safeguarding and the Care Act (2014): the impacts on partnerships and practice', *The Journal of Adult Protection*, 19(4): 209–19.

Cooper, A., Briggs, M., Lawson, J., Hodson, B. and Wilson, M. (2016) *Making Safeguarding Personal: Temperature Check 2016*, London: Association of Directors of Adult Social Services.

Cooper, A., Cocker, C. and Briggs, M. (2018) 'Making Safeguarding Personal and social work practice with older adults: findings from local authority survey data in England', *The British Journal of Social Work*, 48(4): 1014–32.

Cooper, C., Dow, B., Hay, S., Livingston, D. and Livingston, G. (2013) 'Care workers' abusive behavior to residents in care homes: a qualitative study of types of abuse, barriers, and facilitators to good care and development of an instrument for reporting of abuse anonymously', *International Psychogeriatrics*, 25(5): 733–41.

CQC (Care Quality Commission) (2022) 'About us'. Available from: www.cqc.org.uk/about-us

Crath, R., Dixon, J and Warner, J. (2023) 'Risk at the boundaries of social work: an editorial', *Health, Risk & Society*, 25(1-2): 1–8.

Cure the NHS (nd) 'Cure the NHS home page'. Avalable from: www.curethenhs.co.uk

D'Cruz, H. (2004) *Constructing Meanings and Identities in Child Protection Practice*, Melbourne: Tertiary Press.

Dean, M. (2010) *Governmentality: Power and Rule in Modern Society* (2nd edn), London: Sage.

Defert, D. (1991) '"Popular life" and insurance technology', in G. Burchell, C. Gordon and P. Miller (eds) *The Foucault Effect: Studies in Governmentality*, Chicago: University of Chicago Press, pp 211–34.

Delamont, S. (1992) *Fieldwork in Educational Settings*, London: The Falmer Press.

Department for Constitutional Affairs (2004) *The Government Response to the Scrutiny Committee's Report on the Draft Mental Incapacity Bill*, Cm 6121, London: The Stationery Office.

Department of Health (1989) *Caring for People: Community Care in the Next Decade and Beyond*, Cm 849, London: HMSO.

Department of Health (2000) *No Secrets: Guidance on Developing and Implementing Multi-agency Policies and Procedures to Protect Vulnerable Adults from Abuse*, London: Department of Health.

Department of Health (2002) *Fair Access to Care Services: Guidance on Eligibility Criteria for Adult Social Care*, London: Department of Health.

Department of Health (2008a) *Safeguarding Adults: A Consultation on the Review of the 'No Secrets' Guidance*, London: Department of Health.

Department of Health (2008b) *Safeguarding Adults: Report on the Consultation on the Review of 'No Secrets'*, London: Department of Health.

Department of Health (2009) *Best Practice in Managing Risk: Principles and Evidence for Best Practice in the Assessment and Management of Risk to Self and Others in Mental Health Services*, London: Department of Health.

Department of Health (2011) *Caring for Our Future: Shared Ambitions for Care and Support*, London: Department of Health.

Department of Health (2013) *Government Response to the Safeguarding Power of Entry Consultation*, London: Department of Health.

Department of Health and Social Security (1973) *Report of the Committee on Hospital Complaint Procedures*, London: Department of Health and Social Security.

Department of Health and Social Services Inspectorate (1993) *No Longer Afraid: The Safeguard of Older People in Domestic Settings*, London: HMSO.

DHSC (Department of Health and Social Care) (2022) *Care and Support Statutory Guidance*. Available from: www.gov.uk/government/publications/care-act-statutory-guidance/care-and-support-statutory-guidance

Dixon, J. (2012) 'Mentally disordered offenders' views of "their" risk assessment and management plans: perceptions of health risks', *Health, Risk & Society*, 14(7–8): 667–80.

Dixon, J. (2015) 'Treatment, deterrence or labelling: mentally disordered offenders' perspectives on social control', *Sociology of Health & Illness*, 37(8): 1299–1313.

Dixon, J. (2018) 'Narratives of illness and offending: mentally disordered offenders' views on their offending', *Sociology of Health & Illness*, 40(6): 1053–68.

Dixon, J. (2021) *Supporting People Living with Dementia to be Involved in Adult Safeguarding Enquiries*, London: Department of Health and Social Care.

Dixon, J. and Robb, M. (2016) 'Working with women with a learning disability experiencing domestic abuse: how social workers can negotiate competing definitions of risk', *The British Journal of Social Work*, 46(3): 773–88.

Dixon, J., Donnelly, S., Campbell, J. and Laing, J. (2022) 'Safeguarding people living with dementia: how social workers can use supported decision-making strategies to support the human rights of individuals during adult safeguarding enquiries', *The British Journal of Social Work*, 52(3): 1307–24.

Donnelly, S., O'Brien, M., Walsh, J., McInerney, J., Campbell, J. and Kodate, N. (2017) *Adult Safeguarding Legislation and Policy Rapid Realist Literature Review*, Dublin: University College Dublin.

Dons, G., Naert, J. and Roose, R. (2022) 'Transparency in social work: mapping polarities faced by social workers', *The British Journal of Social Work*, 52(8): 5066–83.

Doody, O., Butler, M.P., Lyons, R. and Newman, D. (2017) 'Families' experiences of involvement in care planning in mental health services: an integrative literature review', *Journal of Psychiatric and Mental Health Nursing*, 24(6): 412–30.

Douglas, M. (1966) *Purity and Danger: An Analysis of Concepts of Pollution and Taboo*, London: Routledge.

Douglas, M. (1982) 'Cultural bias', in *In the Active Voice*, London: Routledge & Kegan Paul, pp 183–254.

Douglas, M. (1992) *Risk and Blame: Essays in Cultural Theory*, London: Routledge.

Douglas, M. and Wildavsky, A. (1982) *Risk and Culture: An Essay on the Selection of Technological and Environmental Dangers*, Berkeley, CA: University of California Press.

Doyle, M. and Dolan, M. (2002) 'Violence risk assessment: combining actuarial and clinical information to structure clinical judgements for the formulation and management of risk', *Journal of Psychiatric and Mental Health Nursing*, 9(6): 649–57.

Duffy, S. (2010) 'The citizenship theory of social justice: exploring the meaning of personalisation for social workers', *Journal of Social Work Practice*, 24(3): 253–67.

Dutton, D. (1997) *British Politics Since 1945: The Rise, Fall, and Rebirth of Consensus*, Oxford: Blackwell.

Dwyer, S.C. and Buckle, J.L. (2009) 'The space between: on being an insider-outsider in qualitative research', *International Journal of Qualitative Methods*, 8(1): 54–63.

Eastman, M. (1980) 'The battering of Mrs. Scarfe', *New Age*, 13: 17–19.

Eastman, M. (1982) 'Granny battering, a hidden problem', *Community Care*, 413: 27.

Eastman, M. (1984) *Old Age Abuse*, Mitcham: Age Concern England.

Eastman, M. and Sutton, M. (1982) 'Granny battering', *Geriatric Medicine*, 12(11): 11–15.

Ewald, F. (1991) 'Insurance and risk', in G. Burchell, C. Gordon and P. Miller (eds) *The Foucault Effect: Studies in Governmentality*, Chicago: University of Chicago Press, pp 197–210.

Featherstone, B., Gupta, A., Morris, K. and Warner, J. (2018) 'Let's stop feeding the risk monster: towards a social model of child protection', *Families, Relationships and Societies*, 17(1): 7–22.

Featherstone, B., Gupta, A., Morris, K. and White, S. (2019) *Protecting Children: A Social Model*, Bristol: Policy Press.

Felton, A., Wright, N. and Stacey, G. (2017) 'Therapeutic risk-taking: a justifiable choice', *BJPsych Advances*, 23(2): 81–8.

Ferguson, I. (2007) 'Increasing user choice or privatizing risk? The antinomies of personalization', *The British Journal of Social Work*, 37(3): 387–403.

Ferguson, I. (2012) 'Personalisation, social justice and social work: a reply to Simon Duffy', *Journal of Social Work Practice*, 26(1): 55–73.

Filinson, R. (2007) '"No secrets" and beyond: recent elder abuse policy in England', *Journal of Elder Abuse & Neglect*, 18(1): 1–18.

Finlay, L. (2002) '"Outing" the researcher: the provenance, process, and practice of reflexivity', *Qualitative Health Research*, 12(4): 531–45.

Fitzgerald, G. (2016) 'Care Act guidance on safeguarding must be clearer to ensure victims are protected', *Community Care*, 31 March. Available from: www.communitycare.co.uk/2016/03/31/care-act-guidance-safeguarding-must-clearer-ensure-victims-protected/

Flynn, M. (2012) *Winterbourne View Hospital: A Serious Case Review*, South Gloucestershire: South Gloucestershire Safeguarding Adults Board.

Forrester-Jones, R., Beecham, J., Randall, A., Harrison, R., Malli, M., Sams, L. and Murphy, G. (2020) *Becoming Less Eligible? Intellectual Disability Services in the Age of Austerity*, London: NIHR.

Foucault, M. (1991) 'Governmentality', in G. Burchell, C. Gordon and P. Miller (eds) *The Foucault Effect: Studies in Governmentality*, Chicago: Chicago University Press, pp 87–104.

Francis, R. (2013) *Report of the Mid Staffordshire NHS Foundation Trust Public Inquiry: Executive Summary*, HC 947, London: The Stationery Office.

Fyson, R. (2015) 'Building an evidence base for adult safeguarding? Problems with the reliability and validity of adult safeguarding databases', *The British Journal of Social Work*, 45(3): 932–48.

Fyson, R., Kitson, D. and Corbett, A. (2004) 'Learning disability, abuse and inquiry', in N. Stanley and J. Manthorpe (eds) *The Age of the Inquiry: Learning and Blaming in Health and Social Care*, Routledge: London, pp 215–30.

Gale, N., Dowswell, G., Greenfield, S. and Marshall, T. (2017) 'Street-level diplomacy? Communicative and adaptive work at the front line of implementing public health policies in primary care', *Social Science & Medicine*, 177: 9–18.

Gale, N., Thomas, G.M., Thwaites, R., Greenfield, S. and Brown, P. (2016) 'Towards a sociology of risk work: a narrative review and synthesis', *Sociology Compass*, 10(11): 1046–71.

Giddens, A. (1990) *The Consequences of Modernity*, Stanford, CA: Stanford University Press.

Giddens, A. (1998) *The Third Way: The Renewal of Social Democracy*, Oxford: Polity Press.

Godin, P. (2004) '"You don't tick boxes on a form": a study of how community mental health nurses assess and manage risk', *Health, Risk & Society*, 6(4): 347–60.

Gov.uk (2013) 'Francis report: PM statement on Mid Staffs Public Inquiry'. Available from: www.gov.uk/government/speeches/francis-report-pm-statement-on-mid-staffs-public-inquiry

Gov.uk (2020a) 'Ethnicity facts and figures: age groups', Available from: www.ethnicity-facts-figures.service.gov.uk/uk-population-by-ethnic ity/demographics/age-groups/latest#:~:text=Main%20facts%20and%20 figures%20at%20the%20time%20of,Mixed%20group%20had%20the%20 lowest%2C%20at%2018%20years

Gov.uk (2020b) 'Ethnicity facts and figures: population of England and Wales by ethnicity'. Available from: www.ethnicity-facts-figures.service.gov.uk/ uk-population-by-ethnicity/national-and-regional-populations/population-of-england-and-wales/latest#:~:text=according%20to%20the%202011%20 Census%2C%20the%20total%20population,%28at%202.2%25%29%20 and%20Other%20ethnic%20groups%20%28at%201.0%25%29

Graham, K., Stevens, M., Norrie, C., Manthorpe, J., Moriarty, J. and Hussein, S. (2017) 'Models of safeguarding in England: identifying important models and variables influencing the operation of adult safeguarding', *Journal of Social Work*, 17(3): 255–76.

Green, D. (2007) 'Risk and social work practice', *Australian Social Work*, 60(4): 395–409.

Green, D. and Sawyer, A. (2010) 'Managing risk in community care of older people: perspectives from the frontline', *Australian Social Work*, 63(4): 375–90.

Greengross, S. (1986) *The Law and Vulnerable Elderly People*, Mitcham: Age Concern England.

Grove, W.M. and Meehl, P.E. (1996) 'Comparative efficiency of informal (subjective, impressionistic) and formal (mechanical, algorithmic) prediction procedures: the clinical–statistical controversy', *Psychology, Public Policy, and Law*, 2(2): 293–323.

Hammersley, M. and Atkinson, P. (2019) *Ethnography: Principles in Practice* (4th edn), London: Routledge.

Hannah-Moffat, K. (2005) 'Criminogenic needs and the transformative risk subject: hybridizations of risk/need in penality', *Punishment & Society*, 7(1): 29–51.

Hansard (1965) 'Community Care', HL Deb 07 July 1965 vol 267 cc1332-410. Available from: https://api.parliament.uk/historic-hansard/lords/1965/jul/07/community-care-1

Hansard (1990) 'Beverley Lewis', HC Deb 26 July 1990 vol 177 cc431–2W. Available from: https://api.parliament.uk/historic-hansard/written-answ ers/1990/jul/26/beverley-lewis

Hansard (1997) 'Longcare Homes', HC Deb 2 June 1997 vol 295 c41W. Available from: https://api.parliament.uk/historic-hansard/written-answers/1997/jun/02/longcare-homes

Hardiker, P. (1994) 'Book review: *It could never happen here! The prevention and treatment of sexual abuse of adults with learning disabilities in residential settings*', *Disability & Society*, 9(4): 560–62.

Hardy, M. (2015) *Governing Risk: Care and Control in Contemporary Social Work*, Basingstoke: Palgrave MacMillan.

Hardy, M. (2017) 'In defence of actuarialism: interrogating the logic of risk in social work practice', *Journal of Social Work Practice*, 31(4): 395–410.

Hardy, M. (2020) 'Claim, blame, shame: how risk undermines authenticity in social work', in L. Frost, V. Magyar-Haas, H. Schoneville and A. Sicora (eds) *Shame and Social Work: Theory, Reflexivity and Practice*, Bristol: Policy Press, pp 163–86.

Harris, J. (2022) 'Neoliberal social work and digital technology', in S. Webb (ed) *The Routledge Handbook of International Critical Social Work*, London: Routledge, pp 135–47.

Health and Social Care Act 2008, c 14. Available from: www.legislation.gov.uk/ukpga/2008/14/contents

Hernandez, T.A. (2021) 'The consequences of the austerity policies for public services in the UK', *Studies in Social Justice*, 15(3): 518–37.

Hertfordshire Safeguarding Adults Board (2017) *Making Safeguarding Personal Survey – Results Jan 2017 to October 2017*, Hertfordshire: Hertfordshire Safeguarding Adults Board.

Hewitt, S.E.K. (1987) 'The abuse of deinstitutionalised persons with mental handicaps', *Disability, Handicap & Society*, 2(2): 127–35.

Heyman, B., Alaszewski, A. and Brown, P. (2012) 'Health care through the "lens of risk" and the categorisation of health risks – an editorial', *Health, Risk & Society*, 14(2): 107–15.

Heyman, B., Godin, P.M., Reynolds, L. and Davies, J.P. (2013) 'Assessing the probability of patients reoffending after discharge from low to medium secure forensic mental health services: an inductive prevention paradox', *Health, Risk & Society*, 15(1): 84–102.

Heyman, B., Shaw, M., Davies, J., Godin, P. and Reynolds, L. (2004) 'Forensic mental health services as a risk escalator: a case study of ideals and practice', *Health, Risk & Society*, 6(4): 307–25.

Hilton, C. (2017a) *Improving Psychiatric Care for Older People: Barbara Robb's Campaign 1965–1975*, Houndmills: Palgrave McMillan.

Hilton, C. (2017b) '*Sans Everything* and *The Lancet*: 50 years on', *The Lancet Psychiatry*, 4(2): 104–6.

HM Government (2004) *The Government's Response to the Conclusions of The Health Select Committee's Inquiry into Elder Abuse*, London: The Stationery Office.

HM Government (2007) *Putting People First: A Shared Vision and Commitment to the Transformation of Adult Social Care*, London: The Stationery Office.

HM Government (2012) *Draft Care and Support Bill*, Cm 8386, London: The Stationery Office.

Hollomotz, A. (2014) 'Are we valuing people's choices now? Restrictions to mundane choices made by adults with learning difficulties', *The British Journal of Social Work*, 44(2): 234–51.

Holmes, D. (2013) 'Mid Staffordshire scandal highlights NHS cultural crisis', *The Lancet*, 381(9866), 521–2.

Horlick-Jones, T. (2005) 'Informal logics of risk: contingency and modes of practical reasoning', *Journal of Risk Research*, 8: 253–272.

Horlick-Jones, T. (2005) 'On "risk work": professional discourse, accountability, and everyday action', *Health, Risk & Society*, 7(3): 293–307.

Horlick-Jones, T., Rosenhead, J., Georgiou, I., Ravetz, J. and Löfstedt, R. (2001) 'Decision support for organisational risk management by problem structuring', *Health, Risk & Society*, 3: 141–165.

Horrocks, C. (2000) 'VOICE UK: Support for people with learning disabilities who have been abused', *The Journal of Adult Protection*, 2(4): 36–8.

House of Commons Health Committee (2004) *Elder Abuse: Second Report of Session 2003–04, Volume 1* HC Paper 111-I, London: The Stationery Office.

House of Lords Select Committee on the Mental Capacity Act 2005 (2014) *Mental Capacity Act 2005: Post-legislative Scrutiny*, HL Paper 139, London: The Stationery Office.

Hyslop, I. and Keddell, E. (2018) 'Outing the elephants: exploring a new paradigm for child protection social work', *Social Sciences*, 7(7): 105.

Independent Grenfell Recovery Taskforce (2017) The Taskforce Initial Report. Available from: https://assets.publishing.service.gov.uk/governm ent/uploads/system/uploads/attachment_data/file/949756/171031_ Independent_Grenfell_Recovery_Taskforce_initial_report.pdf

Johnson, D. (2008) 'Strengthening the law to protect vulnerable adults', *Working with Older People*, 12(1): 27–30.

Joint Committee on the Draft Mental Incapacity Bill (2003) *Draft Mental Incapacity Bill: Session 2002–03, Volume 1*, HL Paper 189-1, HC Paper 1083-1, London: The Stationery Office.

Jones, R. (2018) *In Whose Interest? The Privatisation of Child Protection and Social Work*, Bristol: Policy Press.

Juhila, K. and Raitakari, S. (2016) 'Responsibilisation in governmentality literature', in K. Juhila, S. Raitakari and C. Hall (eds) *Responsibilisation at the Margins of Welfare Services*, Abingdon: Routledge, pp 11–34.

Kelly, C. and Quick, O. (2019) 'The legal duty of candour in healthcare: the lessons of history?', *Northern Ireland Legal Quarterly*, 70(1): 77–92.

Kemshall, H. (2001) *Risk, Social Policy and Welfare*, Buckingham: Open University Press.

Kemshall, H. (2010) 'Risk rationalities in contemporary social work policy and practice', *The British Journal of Social Work*, 40(4): 1247–62.

Kemshall, H. (2013) 'Risk assessment and risk management', in M. Davies (ed) *The Blackwell Companion to Social Work* (3rd edn), London: Wiley, pp 333–42.

Kemshall, H. (2014) 'Conflicting rationalities of risk: disputing risk in social policy – reflecting on 35 years of researching risk', *Health, Risk & Society*, 16(5): 398–416.

Kemshall, H. (2016) 'Risk, social policy, welfare and social work', in A. Burgess, A. Alemanno and J. Zinn (eds) *Routledge Handbook of Risk Studies*, London: Routledge, pp 270–9.

Kemshall, H., Parton, N., Walsh, M. and Waterson, J. (1997) 'Concepts of risk in relation to organizational structure and functioning within the personal social services and probation', *Social Policy & Administration*, 31(3): 213–32.

Kemshall, H., Wilkinson, B. and Baker, K. (2013) *Working with Risk: Skills for Contemporary Social Work Practice*, Cambridge: Polity.

Kirin, C. (2016) 'How three conversations have changed the way we do social work', *Community Care*, 3 May. Available from: www.communityc are.co.uk/2016/05/03/three-conversations-changed-way-social-work/

Koehler, J. (2015) *Care and Continuity: Contingency Planning for Provider Failure, A Guide for Local Authorities*, London: LGIU.

Kvale, S. (1996) *InterViews: An Introduction to Qualitative Research Interviewing*, Thousand Oaks, CA: Sage.

Lauder, W., Anderson, I. and Barclay, A. (2003) *Housing and Self-neglect: Carer's and Client's Perspectives*, Swindon: Economic and Social Research Council.

Law Commission (1995) *Mental Incapacity*, Law Com No 231, London: Law Commission.

Law Commission (2010) *Adult Social Care: A Consultation Paper*, London: Law Commission.

LGA (Local Government Association) (2019) *Making Decisions on the Duty to Carry Out Safeguarding Adults Enquiries*, London: Local Government Association.

LGA (Local Government Association) (2021) 'COVID-19 adult safeguarding insight project - second report (July 2021)'. Available from: www.local. gov.uk/publications/covid-19-adult-safeguarding-insight-project-second-report-july-2021

LGA (Local Government Association) (2022a) 'Making Safeguarding Personal Outcomes Framework'. Available from: www.local.gov.uk/mak ing-safeguarding-personal-outcomes-framework

LGA (Local Government Association) (2022b) 'Making Safeguarding Personal Toolkit'. Available from: www.local.gov.uk/msp-toolkit

LGA (Local Government Association) and ADASS (Association of Directors of Adult Social Services) (2018) *Briefing on Working with Risk for Safeguarding Adults Boards*, London: Local Government Association.

LGA (Local Government Association) and ADASS (Association of Directors of Adult Social Services) (2019) *Making Safeguarding Personal: Practice Toolkit Handbook*, London: Local Government Association.

Linsley, P.M. and Shrives, P.J. (2009) 'Mary Douglas, risk and accounting failures', *Critical Perspectives on Accounting*, 20(4): 492–508.

Lord Chancellor (1997) *Who Decides? Making Decisions on Behalf of Mentally Incapacitated Adults: A Consultation Paper Issued by the Lord Chancellor's Department*, London: The Stationery Office.

Lupton, D. (1999) *Risk*, London: Routledge.

Lymbery, M. (2014) 'Social work and personalisation: fracturing the bureau-professional compact?', *The British Journal of Social Work*, 44(4): 795–811.

MacLeod, G. (2018) 'The Grenfell Tower atrocity: exposing urban worlds of inequality, injustice, and an impaired democracy', *City*, 22(4): 460–89.

Manthorpe, J. and Martineau, S. (2015) 'What can and cannot be learned from serious case reviews of the care and treatment of adults with learning disabilities in England? Messages for social workers', *The British Journal of Social Work*, 45(1): 331–48.

Manthorpe, J. and Stevens, M. (2015) 'Adult safeguarding policy and law: A thematic chronology relevant to care homes and hospitals', *Social Policy and Society*, 14(2): 203–16.

Manthorpe, J., Harris, J., Stevens, M. and Moriarty, J. (2018) '"We're effectively becoming immigration officers": social care managers' experiences of the risk work of employing migrant care workers', *Health, Risk & Society*, 20(3–4): 113–25.

Manthorpe, J., Samsi, K. and Rapaport, J. (2013) '"Capacity is key": investigating new legal provisions in England and Wales for adult safeguarding', *Journal of Elder Abuse & Neglect*, 25(4): 355–73.

Manthorpe, J., Stevens, M., Samsi, K., Aspinal, F., Woolham, J. and Hussein, S., et al (2015) 'Did anyone notice the transformation of adult social care? An analysis of Safeguarding Adult Board Annual Reports', *The Journal of Adult Protection*, 17(1): 19–30.

Marczak, J., Fernandez, J.L., Manthorpe, J., Brimblecombe, N., Moriarty, J., Knapp, M. and Snell, T. (2022) 'How have the Care Act 2014 ambitions to support carers translated into local practice? Findings from a process evaluation study of local stakeholders' perceptions of Care Act implementation', *Health and Social Care in the Community*, 30(5): e1711–e1720.

Mathew, D., Brown, H., Kingston, P. and McCreadie, C. (2002) 'The response to "No Secrets"', *The Journal of Adult Protection*, 4(1): 4–14.

May-Chahal, C. and Antrobus, R. (2012) 'Engaging community support in safeguarding adults from self-neglect', *The British Journal of Social Work*, 42(8): 1478–94.

McAdam, D. (2000) 'Culture and social movements', in L.C. Crothers (ed) *Culture and Politics*, New York: Palgrave MacMillan, pp 253–68.

McCreadie, C. (1991) *Elder Abuse: An Exploratory Study*, London: Age Concern Institute of Gerontology, Kings College London.

McCreadie, C. (1993) 'From granny battering to elder abuse: a critique of UK writing, 1975–1992', *Journal of Elder Abuse & Neglect*, 5(2): 7–25.

McCreadie, C., Mathew, D., Filinson, R. and Askham, J. (2008) 'Ambiguity and cooperation in the implementation of adult protection policy', *Social Policy & Administration*, 42(3): 248–66.

McDonald, A. (2010) 'The impact of the 2005 Mental Capacity Act on social workers' decision making and approaches to the assessment of risk', *The British Journal of Social Work*, 40(4): 1229–46.

McKee, K. (2009) 'Post-Foucauldian governmentality: what does it offer critical social policy analysis? *Critical Social Policy*, 29(3): 465–86.

McNeill, F., Burns, N., Halliday, S., Hutton, N. and Tata, C. (2009) 'Risk, responsibility and reconfiguration: penal adaptation and misadaptation', *Punishment & Society*, 11(4): 419–42.

McNicoll, A. and Carter, R. (2016) 'Care Act triggers surge in safeguarding cases', Community Care, 16 March. Available from: www.communityc are.co.uk/2016/03/16/care-act-triggers-surge-safeguarding-caseloads/

Mental Capacity Act 2005, c 9. Available from: www.legislation.gov.uk/ukpga/2005/9/contents

Mental Health Act 1983, c 20. Available from: www.legislation.gov.uk/ukpga/1983/20/contents

Mental Health Act 2007, c12. Available from: www.legislation.gov.uk/ukpga/2007/12/contents

Miller, P. and Rose, N. (2008) *Governing the Present*, Cambridge: Polity Press.

Milner, J.S. and Campbell, J.C. (1995) 'Prediction issues for practitioners', in J. Campbell (ed) *Assessing Dangerousness: Violence by Sexual Offenders, Batterers and Child Abusers*, London: Sage, pp 33–54.

Morriss, L. (2016a) 'AMHP work: dirty or prestigious? Dirty work designations and the approved mental health professional', *The British Journal of Social Work*, 46(3): 703–18.

Morriss, L. (2016b) 'Dirty secrets and being "strange": using ethnomethodology to move beyond familiarity', *Qualitative Research*, 16(5): 526–40.

Morriss, L. (2017) 'Being seconded to a mental health trust: the (in)visibility of mental health social work', *The British Journal of Social Work*, 47(5): 1344–60.

Munro, E. (2004) 'Mental health tragedies: investigating beyond human error', *Journal of Forensic Psychiatry & Psychology*, 15(3): 475–93.

Murphy, D., Duggan, M. and Joseph, S. (2013) 'Relationship-based social work and its compatibility with the person-centred approach: principled versus instrumental perspectives', *The British Journal of Social Work*, 43(4): 703–19.

National Assistance Act 1948, c 29. Available from: www.legislation.gov.uk/ukpga/Geo6/11-12/29/contents/enacted

National Health Service and Community Care Act 1990, c 19. Available from: www.legislation.gov.uk/ukpga/1990/19/contents

NHS Digital (2020) 'Safeguarding Adults England, 2019–20'. Available from: https://digital.nhs.uk/data-and-information/publications/statistical/safeguarding-adults/2019-20

NHS Digital (2022) 'Safeguarding Adults, England, 2021–22', 25 August. Available from: https://digital.nhs.uk/data-and-information/publications/statistical/safeguarding-adults/2021-22

Ogg, J. and Bennett, G. (1992) 'Elder abuse in Britain', *BMJ: British Medical Journal*, 305(6860): 998–9.

Ogilvie, K. and Williams, C. (2010) *Making Safeguarding Personal: A Toolkit for Responses*, London: Local Government Association.

O'Keeffe, M., Hills, A., Doyle, M., McCreadie, C., Scholes, S. and Constantine, R., et al (2007) UK Study of Elder Abuse and Neglect of Older People: Prevalence Survey Report, London: National Centre for Social Research.

O'Malley, P. (2009) 'Responsibilization', in A. Wakefield and J. Fleming (eds) *The SAGE Dictionary of Policing*, London: Sage, pp 277–9.

O'Reilly, K. (2012) *Ethnographic Methods*, London: Routledge.

Parton, N. (1979) 'The natural history of child abuse: a study in social problem definition', *The British Journal of Social Work*, 9(4): 431–51.

Parton, N. (1996) 'Social work, risk and "the blaming system"', in N. Parton (ed) *Social Theory, Social Change and Social Work*, London: Routledge, pp 98–114.

Parton, N. (2008) 'Changes in the form of knowledge in social work: from the "social" to the "informational"?' *The British Journal of Social Work*, 38(2): 253–69.

Penhale, B. and Kingston, P. (1995) 'Social perspectives on elder abuse', in B. Penhale and P. Kingston (eds) *Family Violence and the Caring Professions*, London: Macmillan, pp 222–44.

Perron, B.E., Taylor, H.O., Glass, J.E. and Margerum-Leys, J. (2010) 'Information and communication technologies in social work', *Advances in Social Work*, 11(2): 67–81.

Petersen, A. (2002) 'Risk, governance and the new public health', in A. Petersen and R. Buntin (eds) *Foucault, Health and Medicine*, London: Taylor & Francis, pp 189–206.

Pithouse, A. (2019) *Social Work: The Social Organisation of an Invisible Trade* (2nd edn), London: Routledge.

Pithouse, A., Broadhurst, K., Hall, C., Peckover, S., Wastell, D. and White, S. (2012) 'Trust, risk and the (mis)management of contingency and discretion through new information technologies in children's services', *Journal of Social Work*, 12(2): 158–78.

Pollack, S. (2010) 'Labelling clients "risky": social work and the neo-liberal welfare state', *The British Journal of Social Work*, 40(4): 1263–78.

Preston-Shoot, M. (2018) 'Learning from safeguarding adult reviews on self-neglect: addressing the challenge of change', *The Journal of Adult Protection*, 20(2): 78–92.

Preston-Shoot, M. (2019) 'Self-neglect and safeguarding adult reviews: towards a model of understanding facilitators and barriers to best practice', *The Journal of Adult Protection*, 21(4): 219–34.

Preston-Shoot, M. (2020) 'Safeguarding adult reviews: informing and enriching policy and practice on self-neglect', *The Journal of Adult Protection*, 22(4): 199–215.

Preston-Shoot, M., O'Donoghue, F. and Binding, J. (2022) 'Hope springs: further learning on self-neglect from safeguarding adult reviews and practice', *The Journal of Adult Protection*, 24(3/4): 161–78.

Punch, K.F. (2014) *Introduction to Social Research: Quantitative and Qualitative Approaches* (3rd edn), London: Sage.

Raitakari, S., Juhila, K. and Räsänen, J.-M. (2019) 'Responsibilisation, social work and inclusive social security in Finland', *European Journal of Social Work*, 22(2): 264–76.

Rayner, S. (1992) 'Cultural theory and risk analysis', in S. Krimsky and D. Golding (eds) *Social Theories of Risk*, Westport: Praeger, pp 83–115.

Redley, M., Jennings, S., Holland, A. and Clare, I. (2015) 'Making adult safeguarding personal', *The Journal of Adult Protection*, 17(3): 195–204.

Rex, B. and Campbell, P. (2022) 'The impact of austerity measures on local government funding for culture in England', *Cultural Trends*, 31(1): 23–46.

Robb, B. (1967) *Sans Everything: A Case to Answer*, London: Nelson.

Robb, M. (2021) *Social Workers' Conceptualisations of Domestic Violence and Abuse against People with Learning Disabilities*, Kent: University of Kent.

Robb, M. and McCarthy, M. (2023) 'Managing risk: social workers' intervention strategies in cases of domestic abuse against people with learning disabilities', *Health, Risk & Society*, 25(1-2): 45–60.

Roberts, S.L. (2019) 'Big data, algorithmic governmentality and the regulation of pandemic risk', *European Journal of Risk Regulation*, 10(1): 94–115.

Robertson, J.P. and Collinson, C. (2011) 'Positive risk taking: whose risk is it? An exploration in community outreach teams in adult mental health and learning disability services', *Health, Risk & Society*, 13(2): 147–64.

Robinson, A.L., Rees, A. and Dehaghani, R. (2019) 'Making connections: a multi-disciplinary analysis of domestic homicide, mental health homicide and adult practice reviews', *The Journal of Adult Protection*, 21(1): 16–26.

Rogowski, S. (2011) 'Managers, managerialism and social work with children and families: the deformation of a profession?', *Practice*, 23(3): 157–67.

Rose, N. (1989) *Governing the Soul: The Shaping of the Private Self*, London: Free Association Books.

Rose, N. (1996) 'The death of the social? Re-figuring the territory of government', *International Journal of Human Resource Management*, 25(3): 327–56.

Rose, N. (1999) *Powers of Freedom: Reframing Political Thought*, Cambridge: Cambridge University Press.

Rose, N., O'Malley, P. and Valverde, M. (2006) 'Governmentality', *Annual Review of Law and Social Sciences*, 2: 83–104.

Rothstein, H. (2006) 'The institutional origins of risk: a new agenda for risk research', *Health, Risk & Society*, 8(3): 215–21.

Royal Society (1992) *Risk: Analysis, Perception and Management: Report of a Royal Society Study Group*, London: The Royal Society.

Saleeby, D. (2013) *The Strengths Perspective in Social Work Practice* (6th edn), Boston: Pearson.

Scourfield, J. (2002) *Gender and Child Protection*, Houndmills: Palgrave Macmillan.

Scourfield, J. and Coffey, A. (2006) 'Access, ethics and the (re)construction of gender: the case of researcher as suspected "paedophile"', *International Journal of Social Research Methodology*, 9(1): 29–40.

Scourfield, P. (2007) 'Social care and the modern citizen: client, consumer, service user, manager and entrepreneur', *The British Journal of Social Work*, 37(1): 107–22.

Scourfield, P. (2010) 'Going for brokerage: a task of "independent support" or social work?', *The British Journal of Social Work*, 40(3): 858–77.

Seale, J., Nind, M. and Simmons, B. (2013) 'Transforming positive risk-taking practices: the possibilities of creativity and resilience in learning disability contexts', *Scandinavian Journal of Disability Research*, 15(3): 233–48.

Shaw, I., Bell, M., Sinclair, I., Sloper, P., Mitchell, W. and Dyson, P., et al (2009) 'An exemplary scheme? An evaluation of the Integrated Children's System', *The British Journal of Social Work*, 39(4): 613–26.

Simcock, P. and Manthorpe, J. (2014) 'Deafblind and neglected or deafblindness neglected? Revisiting the case of Beverley Lewis', *The British Journal of Social Work*, 44(8): 2325–41.

Sletten, M.S. and Ellingsen, I.T. (2020) 'When standardization becomes the lens of professional practice in child welfare services', *Child & Family Social Work*, 25(3): 714–22.

Smith, M. and Clement, J. (2003) 'The terrible costs of abuse at Longcare Care Home', Available from: www.bucksfreepress.co.uk/news/423905. the-terrible-costs-of-abuse-at-longcare-care-home/

Social Care Institute for Excellence (2016) 'Care Act 2014: data collection and analysis'. Available from: www.scie.org.uk/care-act-2014/safeguarding-adults/safeguarding-adults-boards-checklist-and-resources/quality-assura nce/data-collection-and-analysis.asp#:~:text=Local%20authorities%20 are%20required%20to%20collect%20standard%20data,evaluate%20and%20 regionally%20benchmark%20its%20own%20safeguarding%20performance

Spencer-Lane, T. (2014) *Care Act Manual*, London: Sweet & Maxwell.

Spradley, J.P. (2016a) *The Ethnographic Interview*, Long Grove, IL: Waveland Press.

Spradley, J.P. (2016b) *Participant Observation*, Long Grove, IL: Waveland Press.

Stanley, N. and Manthorpe, J. (2001) 'Reading mental health inquiries: messages for social work', *Journal of Social Work*, 1(1): 77–99.

Stanley, N. and Manthorpe, J. (2004) 'Introduction: the inquiry as Janus', in N. Stanley and J. Manthorpe (eds) *The Age of the Inquiry: Learning and Blaming in Health and Social Care*, London: Routledge, pp 1–16.

Stevens, M., Manthorpe, J., Martineau, S. and Norrie, C. (2020) 'Practice perspectives and theoretical debates about social workers' legal powers to protect adults', *Journal of Social Work*, 20(1): 3–22.

Stevens, M., Woolham, J., Manthorpe, J., Aspinall, F., Hussein, S. and Baxter, K., et al (2018) 'Implementing safeguarding and personalisation in social work: findings from practice', *Journal of Social Work*, 18(1): 3–22.

Stevenson, M. and Taylor, B.J. (2017) 'Risk communication in dementia care: professional perspectives on consequences, likelihood, words and numbers', *The British Journal of Social Work*, 47(7): 1940–58.

Stoltz, D. (2014) 'Diagrams of theory: Douglas and Wildavsky's grid/group typology of worldviews'. Available from: https://dustinstoltz.com/blog/ 2014/06/04/diagram-of-theory-douglas-and-wildavskys-gridgroup-typol ogy-of-worldviews

Sumner, K. (2002) *No Secrets: The Protection of Vulnerable Adults: Findings from an Analysis of Local Codes of Practice*, London: Department of Health.

Sutton, C. (1992) *Confronting Elder Abuse: A Social Services Inspectorate London Region Survey*, London: HMSO.

Taylor, B.J. (2006) 'Risk management paradigms in health and social services for professional decision making on the long-term care of older people', *The British Journal of Social Work*, 36(8): 1411–29.

Taylor, B.J. and McKeown, C. (2013) 'Assessing and managing risk with people with physical disabilities: the development of a safety checklist', *Health, Risk & Society*, 15(2): 162–75.

Taylor, K. and Dodd, K. (2003) 'Knowledge and attitudes of staff towards adult protection', *The Journal of Adult Protection*, 5(4): 26–32.

Teggi, D. (2022) *End of Life Care in English Care Homes: Governance, Care Work and the Good Death*, PhD thesis, University of Bath.

The Care and Support (Eligibility Criteria) Regulations 2015, SI No 313. Available from: www.legislation.gov.uk/uksi/2015/313/contents/made

The Care Homes Regulations 2001, SI 3965. Available from: www.legislation.gov.uk/uksi/2001/3695/contents/made

The Care Quality Commission (Registration) Regulations 2009, SI No 3112. Available from: www.legislation.gov.uk/uksi/2009/3112/contents/made

The Domiciliary Care Agencies Regulations 2002, SI 3214. Available from: www.legislation.gov.uk/uksi/2002/3214/contents/made

Titterton, M. (2004) *Risk and Risk Taking in Health and Social Welfare*, London: Jessica Kingsley Publishers.

Titterton, M. (2011) 'Positive risk taking with people at risk of harm', in H. Kemshall and B. Wilkinson (eds) *Good Practice in Assessing Risk: Current Knowledge, Issues and Approaches*, London: Jessica Kingsley Publishers, pp 30–47.

Tomlin, S. (1989) *Abuse of Elderly People: An Unnecessary and Preventable Problem*, London: British Geriatric Society.

Walshe-Brennan, K. (1977) 'Granny bashing', *Nursing Mirror*, 145(25): 32–4.

Warner, J. (2006) 'Inquiry reports as active texts and their function in relation to professional practice in mental health', *Health, Risk & Society*, 8(3): 223–37.

Warner, J. (2013) 'Social work, class politics and risk in the moral panic over Baby P.', *Health, Risk & Society*, 15(3): 217–33.

Warner, J. (2015) *The Emotional Politics of Social Work and Child Protection*, Bristol: Policy Press.

Warner, J. and Gabe, J. (2008) 'Risk, mental disorder and social work practice: a gendered landscape', *The British Journal of Social Work*, 38(1): 117–34.

Webb, S.A. (2006) *Social Work in a Risk Society: Social and Political Perspectives*, Houndmills: Palgrave MacMillan.

Webb, S.A. (2009) 'Risk, governmentality and insurance: the actuarial recasting of social work', in H.-U. Otto, A. Polutta and H. Ziegler (eds) *Evidence-based Practice: Modernising the Knowledge Base of Social Work?* Opladen and Farmington Hills, MI: Barbara Budrich Publishers, pp 211–26.

Weber, L. and McCulloch, J. (2019) 'Penal power and border control: which thesis? Sovereignty, governmentality, or the pre-emptive state?', *Punishment & Society*, 21(4): 496–514.

Whittington, C. (2016) 'The promised liberation of adult social work under England's 2014 Care Act: genuine prospect or false prospectus?', *The British Journal of Social Work*, 46(7): 1942–61.

Wilkins, A. and Gobby, B. (2022) 'Objects and subjects of risk: a governmentality approach to education governance', *Globalisation, Societies and Education*, 1–14. doi: 10.1080/14767724.2022.2114073.

Williams, C. (1993) 'Vulnerable victims? A current awareness of the victimisation of people with learning disabilities', *Disability, Handicap & Society*, 8(2): 161–72.

Yoeli, H., Lonbay, S.P., Morey, S. and Pizycki, L. (2016) 'Safeguarding adults: from realism to ritual', *The Journal of Adult Protection*, 18(6): 329–40.

Zinn, J.O. (2008) 'Heading into the unknown: everyday strategies for managing risk and uncertainty', *Health, Risk & Society*, 10(5): 439–50.

Zinn, J.O. (2016) '"In-between" and other reasonable ways to deal with risk and uncertainty: A review article', *Health, Risk & Society*, 18(7–8): 348–66.

Zinn, J.O. (2020) 'Responsibilisation: blaming or empowering risk-taking', in J.O. Zinn (ed) *Understanding Risk-taking*, Cham: Springer, pp 225–52.

Index

References to tables appear in **bold** type. Names followed by ★ indicate pseudonyms.

A

abuse
  categories 5, 60, 71, 128, 134, 137
  definitions 21, 24, 26, 32, 54, 56
accountability 51–2, 95, 118–19, 132
Action on Elder Abuse 23, 27, 32
actuarialism 50–1, 100, 130
Adrian★ 75–6, 96, 105, 107–8
adult abuse *see* learning disabled adults;
  older adult abuse; vulnerable adults
adult community teams
  ICT systems 65, 66, 130
  longer-term safeguarding 11, 63–4, **64**,
    86, 88, 130
  proportionality 92
  referrals/assessments 63–5, **64**, 70, 76,
    104, 113
  research process 3, 9, **10**, 11–12
adult safeguarding, history of
  Care Act 2014 1, 4–6
  20th Century 17–26
  21st Century 26–34
Age Concern England 21, 23
Aid for the Elderly in Government
  Institutions (AEGIS) 18, 19
Alice★ 70, 71, 84, 86
Almsbury★ 8, 64, **64**, 87, 100, 113
Amanda★ 91–2, 94, 101
Arnoldi, J. 42
Ash, A. 71
Association for Residential Care (ARC)
  24
Association of Directors of Adult Social
  Services (ADASS) 5, 29, 30, 33
Association of Directors of Social Services
  (ADSS) 27, 28–9
audits 28, 52, 65–6, 67, 69
austerity 83–8, 91, 128, 131, 134, 135

B

Bailey, Julie 31
BBC 31
Beck, Ulrich 37–9, 45, 47, 126
Beech House inquiry 25
Best, J. 16–17, 134
Best Practice in Managing Risk (Department
  of Health, 2009) 51
Beveridge report (1942) 48
blame
  referrals/assessments 75, 78
  risk theories 43, 49

social work practice 22, 51–2, 54–5,
  115, 119, 132
Blumer, H. 16
Boateng, Paul 25
British Geriatrics Society 21
British Medical Journal 20
Brown, P. 46–7, 53, 83, 119–20
Bryan, Terry 31
Buckle, J.L. 12
Burrows, D. 72
Burston, B.J. 20
Butler, I. 19, 47

C

Calnan, M. 119–20
Cameron, David 31
Candice★ 94
Care Act 2014
  adult safeguarding 1, 16, 127, 135,
    137
  care providers 119, 136
  family carers 116, 117
  local authority duties 4–6, 16, 32–4, 60–1,
    89–90, 134
  person-led safeguarding 82, 124
  referrals/assessments 60–2, 70–1, 74, 76,
    77, 133
  safeguarding principles 88–97, 128
  see also safeguarding enquiry criteria
    (Section 42)
care agencies
  business failures 87, 135
  laws/policies 118
  referrals/assessments 73, 90, 102, 103,
    106
  risk assessments by 102, 121–2, 131
Care and Support (Eligibility Criteria)
  Regulations (2015) 90
Care and Support Statutory Guidance
  (DHSC, 2022)
  abuse categories 5, 60, 71, 128, 134, 137
  safeguarding 1, 32–3, 89–97
  see also safeguarding principles, *Care and
    Support Statutory Guidance*
care homes
  CQC reports 92–3, 119, 120, 125, 134
  inquiries 25, 136
  referrals/assessments 62, 64, 72, 75, 103
  self-reporting 75, 94, 119, 120, 136
  social work resourcing 86, 87, 118, 123–4
  see also nursing homes

care plans 3, 36, 49, 57, 121–2, 131
care providers
  referrals/assessments 60, 64, 65, 77
  trust 118–21, 122, 133–4
  see also care homes; care workers;
    nursing homes
Care Quality Commission (CQC)
  Care Act 2014 32
  care providers 92–3, 119, 120, 125, 134
  hospitals 30, 31
Care Standards Act 2000 26, 28
care workers 62, 84, 106, 114, 122–3, 136
carers 61, 104, 116
  see also family carers
Carr, S. 49
Castel, R. 40–1, 65
child abuse 20
child protection 108, 109, 136
Claire★ 60, 62, 68, 76, 90–1, 113
Clements, Luke 32
Collingridge, Graham 27
Colwell, Maria 20
Commission for Social Care Inspection 29
communicating risks 103–4, 107–9,
  115, 133
community care 22, 29, 90
community resources 87–8, 91–2, 93
Complecare★ 84–5
Court of Protection 27, 111, 118
Crossman, Richard 18
cultural theory of risk 42–4, 51
Cure the NHS 30–1

D

decision-making see mental capacity;
  positive risk taking; professional
  judgement/decision-making
defensive practice
  care workers 121
  inappropriate referrals 75, 78, 133
  social workers 3, 52, 54–5, 96, 110
Delamont, S. 3
dementia 5, 29, 62, 88, 104
Department of Health 19, 23, 29, 30
  see also No Secrets (Department of
  Health, 2000)
Department of Health and Social Care
  (DHSC) see Care and Support Statutory
  Guidance (DHSC, 2022); No Longer
  Afraid (DHSC, 1993)
domestic abuse 55, 72, 74, 91, 113–14
Dorrell, Stephen 24
Douglas, Mary 42–3, 45, 51, 75
Drakeford, M. 19, 47
drug abuse 109, 111, 112, 113, 114
Duffy, S. 49
duty of candour 32, 119
duty social workers 63, 64, 70
Dwyer, S.C. 12

E

Eastman, Mervyn 21
Edwards, John 19
elder abuse see older adult abuse
Ely Hospital 18–19
emergency service referrals 74–5
empathy 47, 68, 111, 116, 117, 136
empowerment
  Care Act 2014 5, 82
  community care policies 22
  learning disabled adults 55, 109, 113–14
  Making Safeguarding Personal 54,
    55, 82
  responsibilisation 49
  safeguarding principles 89, 95, 132
ethics 8, 70, 74, 135, 137
ethnography 7–9, 11, 12–13, 68

F

face-to-face assessments 65, 103–4, 113,
  117, 125
Fair Access to Care Services 28, 90, 91
falls 20, 21, 64, 72, 94, 119
family carers 26, 31, 114, 115–18,
  133, 136
financial abuse
  Care Act 2014 32
  empowerment 114
  family carers 117–18
  Mental Capacity Act 2005 28,
    109–10
  prevalence data 23, 29
fire risk referrals 74, 75–6
Fitzgerald, Gary 27, 32, 33
Fosborough★
  interventions 100–1, 104, 113, 117,
    130
  referrals/assessments 61, 63–4, **64**, 66,
    71, 77
  research location 8, 9
  resourcing 86, 87–8, 90–1
Foucault, M. 39
Francis, Robert 31
Friern Hospital 17–18

G

Gabe, J. 56
Gainsborough★
  care provider business failures 84, 135
  referrals/assessments 62, 64, **64**, 66–8,
    100, 113
  research location 8, 9
Gale, N. 46–7, 53, 69, 83, 112
gender **10**, 39, 43, 50, 56
Gibbs, Amy 17–18
Giddens, A. 38
Gloucester Social Services 24
governmentality 39–42, 44–5, 48–9, 130

H

Hannah-Moffat, K. 101
Hardy, M. 52
Harvey, Audrey 18
Hayley* 95–6
Health and Social Care Act 2008 32, 119
Healthcare Commission 30
Hewitt, S.E.K. 22
hoarding 60, 71, 117, 128, 134
Horlick-Jones, Tom 44–5, 60, 65, 127
Hospital Advisory Service 19
hospitals
  ICT systems 68
  inquiries 18–19, 25, 31, 136
  long-stay hospitals 17–18, 22
  loyalty to service users 72
House of Commons Health Committee on Elder Abuse (2004) 27–8
House of Lords 18
House of Lords Select Committee on the Mental Capacity Act 2005 7
housing
  government programmes 48
  professionals 76, 101–2, 105, 109, 122
  quality of 21, 74
  supported 22, 94, 101–2
Howe, Geoffrey 18–19

I

identities 12–13, 37, 39
inappropriate referrals 74–7, 78, 133
information and communication technology (ICT) systems 61, 65–9, 72, 77, 107, 129–30
Ingrid* 95, 101–2, 114
initial assessments 61–5, **64**, 70–2, 87, 106–7
inquiries 2, 18–19, 24, 25, 30, 52
Isobel* 93, 119

J

Jenny* 87, 94
Joint Committee on the Draft Mental Capacity Bill (2003) 26–7

K

Karen* 90
Kemshall, H. 132
Kerry* 92, 120, 121
Kvale, S. 12

L

Law Commission 24–5, 27, 30
laws 21, 54–5
  see also Care Act 2014; Care Standards Act 2000; Health and Social Care Act 2008; Mental Capacity Act 2005; Mental Health Act 1983 and 2007;

National Assistance Act 1948; National Health Service and Community Care Act 1990; statutory duties; statutory powers
learning disabled adults
  empowerment 55, 109, 113–14
  family carers 117
  historical safeguarding 18–19, 22, 24, 25, 31
  risk assessments 51, 103–4
  safeguarding enquiries 75
Lewis, Beverley 22, 24
Lewis, Ivan 29
Lisa* 73, 74, 90, 106, 115–16, 122–3
local authorities
  austerity 83, 84–5, 91, 128, 135
  Care Act 2014 4–6, 32–3, 60–1, 89–90, 134
  care provider business failures 84, 135–6
  decentralisation 49
  historical safeguarding (pre-2014) 23–9
  No Secrets 26–7, 28, 29, 53–4, 60
  resourcing responsibilities 123–4
  safeguarding principles 89–91, 94
  see also Care Act 2014
Local Government Association (LGA) 5, 30, 33, 54, 136
Longcare inquiry 25
Louise* 66, 96
Lush, Denzil 27

M

Making Safeguarding Personal
  evaluations of 55, 136
  LGA/ADASS 5, 30, 33
  social workers' use of 82, 90–1, 104, 128
  toolkits 30, 54, 136
Marcia* 109–10, 117–18
Margaret* 67, 77, 88, 104–5, 111
Mavis* 72, 110
McAdam, D. 30
McCarthy, M. 55, 133
McCreadie, C. 54–5, 56
medication errors 31, 62, 64, 84, 119
Mencap 31
mental capacity
  Mental Capacity Act 2005 6–7, 28, 109–11, 128, 131
  other legislation/reports 24, 26–8, 29
  research findings 87, 101, 103–4
Mental Health Acts 1983 and 2007 3
mental health sector 2–3, 17–18, 20, 40–1, 51, 56
Mid Staffordshire NHS Foundation Trust 30
Mike* 60, 67–8, 69, 77–8, 104, 119
Ministry of Health 18
mistreatment, definition 29
Morriss, Lisa 13

multi-agency work 54, 57, 91–3, 128
multidisciplinary work 3, 21, 28, 56, 101, 131

N

Nadia★ 87, 113, 114
National Assistance Act 1948 27
National Association for the Protection from Sexual Abuse of Adults and Children with Learning Disabilities (NAPSAC) 24
National Health Service and Community Care Act 1990 23, 25
National Health Service (NHS) 19, 23, 24, 25, 34, 93
neglect
  care provider business failures 84
  definitions 56
  historical safeguarding 28–9, 31
  referrals/assessments 70, 76
  see also self-neglect
neoliberalism 41, 48–9, 52, 126, 128
Nicola★ 66–7, 68, 72, 78, 103, 108, 122
No Longer Afraid (DHSC, 1993) 24
No Secrets (Department of Health, 2000) 26–7, 28, 29, 53–4, 60, 127
norms 42, 45, 56, 60, 73
Northern Ireland 54, 55
notifiable safety incidents 32, 119
nurses
  abusive behaviour of 18, 19, 31
  district/community 20, 94
  referrals from 106, 116, 122
nursing homes 56, 73, 75, 77, 93, 118
  see also care homes

O

Office of the Public Guardian 28
Old Age Abuse (Eastman) 21
older adult abuse 20–1, 23–4, 27–9

P

paid carers see care workers
Panorama 31
Panting, Margaret 27
Partners for Change 91
partnership and prevention 93–5, 132
Parton, N. 51
paternalism 7, 82–3, 101, 129
Patricia★ 75, 91, 123–4
Penny★ 109, 121
person-led safeguarding
  Care Act 2014 82, 89–90, 124
  service users' view of risk 111–12
  social workers' perspectives on 102–6
  see also Making Safeguarding Personal
personalisation
  austerity 83–4, 91, 135
  introduction of 29, 30

social work practice 49, 53, 54, 128–9
physical abuse
  care home resident-on-resident 62, 64, 119
  domestic violence 72, 74, 113–14
  hospitals 18–19, 25, 31
  older adults 20–1, 23, 25, 27–9
Pithouse, A. 8
police
  discretion/power 45
  family carers 117
  historical safeguarding 22, 23, 26, 27
  referrals from 62, 68–9
  social relations with social workers 56
positive risk taking
  accountability 96–7
  Making Safeguarding Personal 54–5
  practice models 51, 52
  service users' capacitated decisions 2, 101, 110, 129, 131, 133
powers of attorney 7, 28, 111, 117–18
powers of entry 25, 29, 32, 33, 114–15
Practitioner Alliance against Abuse of Vulnerable Adults 26
pressure sores 25, 62, 90, 100, 119
prevention see partnership and prevention
probability 36, 40–2, 45–6, 50, 53
professional judgement/decision-making
  actuarialism 50–1, 100, 130
  referrals/assessments 45–6, 61–4, 70–7, 100, 101, 103
  safeguarding principles 95–6
  social relations/team cultures 55, 56, 73–4, 77, 129–30
  social work values 48
proportionality 53, 90–3, 94, 131, 132, 135
protection, safeguarding principle 95, 132
psychological abuse 23, 29
public inquiries 24, 30
Purity and Danger (Douglas) 42–3

R

Rachel★ 70–1, 100–1, 111
Ram★ 62
Rebecca★ 77, 103–4
research process
  locations 7–8, 16
  methods 1–4, 7–13, **10**, 16–17
  recommendations 134–7
  researcher's social work experience 2–4, 12–13, 16
residential care 23–6
  see also care homes; nursing homes
resourcing
  care homes/providers 86–7, 118, 123–4, 131, 134
  family carers 115
  safeguarding principles 90–3

responsibilisation 41–2, 46, 48–9,
  100–2, 121–4, 131, 133–4
risk
  definitions 36, 45, 127
  service users' views 111–12
  social work practice 2–3, 36, 47–8, 126
  see also positive risk taking
risk assessments
  by care agencies 102, 121, 122, 131
  governmentality 40–1
  ICT systems 61–5, 68, 72, 129–30
  professional judgement 71–3
  tools 45–6, 50–1, 71, 99–102,
    111–12, 128
  translation, knowledge 46, 69–71, 129
  see also face-to-face assessments; initial
    assessments; telephone assessments
risk interventions, definition/types 53,
  55, 61
risk knowledge
  Care Act 2014 60, 61, 70–1, 82,
    127, 133
  ICT systems 65–9, 77, 129
  risk theories 37–40, 42–3
  social relations 46–7, 74, 77, 82,
    120, 133
  translation 46, 69–71, 88–97, 129, 133
risk theories
  cultural theory of risk 42–4, 51
  governmentality 39–42, 44–5, 48–9, 130
  risk society 37–9, 45, 47, 48
risk work
  referrals/assessments 61, 74, 77, 81
  resourcing 83, 97
  theories/models 44–7, 53–4, 118, 126
Robb, Barbara 17–18
Robb, M. 55, 113, 133
Robinson, Kenneth 18
Rose, N. 40
Rowe, Gordon 25
Royal Society 45

S

safeguarding, definition 1
'safeguarding adults,' term 28–9
Safeguarding Adults (ADSS, 2005) 28–9
Safeguarding Adults Boards 4, 32, 60,
  67, 134
safeguarding enquiries
  after internal investigation 123, 134
  ICT systems 66, 69, 72, 77
  Making Safeguarding Personal 30, 136
  professional judgement 72–3, 75–6
  service users' involvement 107–14, 136
  workload pressures 33, 87, 93
safeguarding enquiry criteria (Section 42)
  explained to service users 109
  inappropriate referrals 74, 76, 77, 133
  overview 4–5

referrals/assessments 60–2, 70–1, 128
  safeguarding principles 93, 94, 97
  statistical data 33–4
safeguarding principles, Care and Support
    Statutory Guidance
  accountability 95–7, 132
  empowerment 89, 95, 132
  partnership and prevention 93–5, 132
  proportionality 53, 90–3, 94, 131,
    132, 135
  protection 95, 132
  wellbeing 89–90, 128, 132
safeguarding referrals
  Care Act 2014 4, 60, 61, 135
  family carers 116
  ICT systems 65–9, 72, 107, 129–30
  inappropriate referrals 74–7, 78, 133
  initial assessments 61–5, **64**, 70–2,
    87, 106–7
  resourcing 33, 84–7, 106–7, 124,
    131, 135
  screening 9, 11, 61–5, **64**, 85–6, 130
  statistics 33–4
  team cultures 73–4, 129–30
safeguarding teams
  ICT systems 65, 66, 130
  referrals/assessments 63–5, **64**, 71, 76,
    113, 130
  research process 9, **10**, 11
  safeguarding principles 90–4
  workload pressures 33, 87, 106–7
Sans Everything (Robb) 17, 18
scientific knowledge 37–8, 42, 45, 53, 128
screening 9, 11, 61–5, **64**, 85–6, 130
self-neglect
  Care Act 2014 32–3, 60, 71, 74,
    128, 134
  Mental Capacity Act 2005 110
  public attitudes 55
self-reporting 75, 94, 119, 120, 136
Sense 24
service users
  insight 113–14
  safeguarding enquiries 107–14, 136
  social relations with social worker 55–6,
    82, 87, 104–9, 132
  see also empowerment; Making
    Safeguarding Personal; person-led
    safeguarding; personalisation; positive
    risk taking; responsibilisation
sex workers 87, 111–12, 114
sexual abuse 24, 29, 60, 104
Simon* 70, 82, 96, 117
Social Care Institute for Excellence 30
social class 37, 39, 43
social relations, social workers'
  with carers 115–20
  risk knowledge 46–7, 74, 77, 82,
    120, 133

with service users 55–6, 82, 87, 104–9, 132
between social work teams 63–5, 79, 87–8
Social Services Inspectorate 23, 24
social workers
  blame 22, 51–2, 54–5, 132
  defensive practice 3, 52, 54–5, 96, 110
  person-led safeguarding, perspective on 102–6
  researcher's role as 2–4, 12–13, 16
  responsibilities 48–9, 54–5, 95–6, 101
  risk, relationship to 2–3, 36, 47–8, 126
  training 16, 54, 134
  values 48, 49, 52, 72, 135
  see also adult community teams; duty social workers; safeguarding teams; social relations, social workers'
Spradley, J.P. 11, 12
Stafford Hospital 31
state responsibilities 41, 46, 49, 83, 100, 131
statistical data
  actuarialism 50–1, 100, 130
  ICT systems 67
  pattern spotting 72–3, 77–8, 129
  probability 36, 40–2, 45–6, 50, 53
  safeguarding figures 33–4
statutory duties 14, 36, 60, 134
statutory guidance see Care and Support Statutory Guidance (DHSC, 2022)
statutory powers
  Care Act 2014 32–4, 128, 135
  of entry 25, 29, 32, 33, 114–15
  lack of 24, 27, 29, 34
  service user engagement 105–6
Stevenson, M. 55
Strabolgi, Lord and Lady 18
strategy meetings 94, 101, 114, 117, 123, 124
supported housing 22, 94, 101–2

T

taboo behaviours 42, 44, 51

Taylor, B.J. 55
team cultures 73–4, 129–30
telephone assessments 68, 103–4, 106, 113, 121, 132
telephone referrals 61, 72, 78, 86–7
thresholds 73, 76, 84, 97, 130, 135
Tooth, Dr Geoffrey 18
training
  care providers 28, 121, 136–7
  social workers 16, 54, 134
translation, knowledge 46, 69–71, 88–97, 129, 133
transparency 32, 49, 95, 107–9, 117, 119
trust
  with care providers 118–21, 122, 133–4
  communicating risks 103, 107–9, 115, 133
  family carers 115, 133
  risk theories 38, 44
  of service users 45–6, 47, 56, 88, 106
  social work values 48

V

Victoria★ 84–5
Voice UK 23
vulnerable adults
  learning disabled adults 22
  No Secrets 26–7, 28, 29, 53–4
  older adults 21, 24
  referrals/assessments 62
  resourcing 87

W

Warner, J. 56
Webb, S.A. 48, 51, 52, 100, 130
welfare policy 48–9, 50–1
wellbeing 89–90, 128, 132
Welsh Assembly Government 30
Williams, John 27
Winterbourne View 31
workload pressures 33, 85–7, 93, 104, 106–7, 131

Z

Zinn, J.O. 128

CPSIA information can be obtained
at www.ICGtesting.com
Printed in the USA
JSHW061317140723
44774JS00002B/36

9 781447 357292